The British Empire

An Enthralling Guide to the Rise and Fall of the World's Largest Superpower in History

Free limited time bonus

Stop for a moment. We have a free bonus set up for you. The problem is this: we forget 90% of everything that we read after 7 days. Crazy fact, right? Here's the solution: we've created a printable, 1-page pdf summary for this book that you're reading now. All you have to do to get your free pdf summary is to go to the following website:

https://livetolearn.lpages.co/enthrallinghistory/

Once you do, it will be intuitive. Enjoy, and thank you!

We forget 90% of everything that we've read in 7 days...

Get the free printable pdf summary of the book you've read AND much, much more... shhhh...

Enter Your Most Frequently Used Email to Get Started

DOWNLOAD FREE PDF SUMMARY

© Enthralling History

Table of Contents

Introduction

Long before countries like the United States or China became global superpowers, Great Britain held the honor and title of being an undeniable world superpower.

For over four hundred years, colonies, states, countries, and territories around the world fell under the sovereignty of the British Crown. In the early 1920s, Britain was the ruler of nearly a quarter of the world, making the nation the largest and one of the most powerful empires in history.

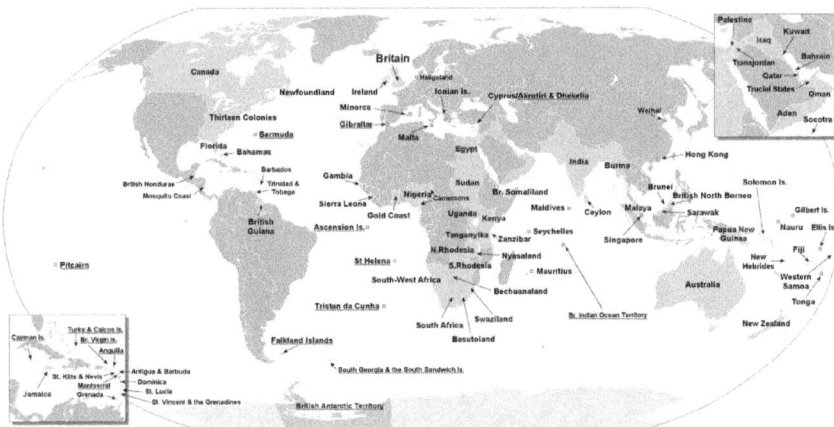

Territories that were part of the British Empire.
RedStorm1368, CC BY-SA 4.0 <https://creativecommons.org/licenses/by-sa/4.0>, via Wikimedia Commons; https://commons.wikimedia.org/wiki/File:The_British_Empire_5.png

How did such an island nation yield so much power and control? Where and how did it start to go wrong? Why did the sun set on the

British Empire?

In this book, we will look at how the empire was established during the Age of Discovery, how it grew and expanded, and the impact and legacy the crumbling empire left behind.

Chapter 1: Britain Discovers Its Empire

The British Empire wasn't discovered or formed overnight. A combination of factors, which included trade, conquest, colonization, diplomacy, and historical events, all helped Britain shape its empire over several centuries.

One of the most significant factors that played a role in the development of the British Empire was trade.

By the late 18th century, following a victorious win in the Seven Years' War, which is often viewed as the world's first global conflict, Britain emerged as a powerful maritime power and was in almost complete control of the world's seas. This, combined with a strong economy, put Britain in a unique position to establish trade networks with other countries around the world.

The East India Company, which was established by the British to help English merchants trade in foreign areas, played a key role in establishing relations with India and other parts of Asia. The transatlantic slave trade was also established to maintain and further British interests, primarily in the Americas and the Caribbean islands.

But it was, without a doubt, colonization that played the biggest role in the building of the empire. British settlers established colonies in various parts of the world, including North America, the Caribbean, Africa, and Asia. These colonies provided Britain with valuable resources and wealth and helped to expand Britain's imperialist agenda.

Britain's power also grew considerably through conquest. Britain was able to acquire new land and territories through military campaigns and its powerful military force. One acquisition or conquest inevitably led to another one, almost like a domino effect.

In addition to using their military force, the British were skilled at diplomacy, which played a key role in the growth of the empire. It would have been nearly impossible for Britain to look after all its colonies without some strategic partnerships.

Knowing this, Britain worked hard at establishing alliances and treaties with other countries, which, in turn, helped to not only expand its influence but also ensured its interests around the world were protected and secure.

Origins of the Empire

Now that we've looked at the ways in *which* Britain built its empire, let's look at *when* it started.

The concept of gaining power and influence through the conquest of land was nothing new by the time the British Empire started. From the earliest days of civilizations, wars and battles were waged over territories and land. Empires like ancient Egypt, ancient Greece, and ancient Rome all conquered lands and established colonies to increase their power and influence.

Even though parts of Africa and Asia had begun to be explored, modern-day colonization is deemed to have begun during the Age of Discovery at the start of the 15th century. In the 1400s, Spain and Portugal explored the regions of Central and South America and looked at expansion in the New World. England soon followed suit. The first English colony was founded in North America when explorer Sir Walter Raleigh built a settlement in Virginia called Roanoke in 1585.

Roanoke lasted for just a couple of years before it disappeared. The mystery of what happened to the residents of Roanoke endures to this day.

After this failed attempt, the development of the British Empire began in earnest with the establishment of Jamestown in 1607 by Captain John Smith and others.

John Smith landing at Jamestown.
https://commons.wikimedia.org/wiki/File:Captain_John_Smith_landing_in_Jamestown.jpeg

By this time, colonialism was well underway, with several European empires racing around the world, conquering and claiming parts of the world for themselves.

With advancements in shipbuilding, mapping, and navigation, it became easier than ever for explorers to travel around the world, leading to the discovery of new lands and countries.

Henry VIII and Colonialism

The Tudor monarchy is perhaps most famous for King Henry VIII, his six wives, the splitting of the Catholic Church, and his children, who went on to rule England. The Tudors are also credited with laying the foundation for English colonialism.

The largest expansion of English territory to take place on the continent of Europe happened under King Henry VIII's rule when he invaded France in the summer of 1544.

Wars with France were nothing new for England. The two countries seemed to be natural-born enemies and locked in a continuous struggle for power and dominance. While medieval monarchs in England wanted to rule France as their king, Henry VIII did something different.

He went to war and successfully captured Boulogne. Then, he annexed the French lands under his own rule and established a colonial settlement.

The annexation would last for six years. Historically, this is not viewed as the beginning of the British Empire; however, it did set the stage and tone for how Britain would expand. This was seen clearly when English colonies were established in Ireland in the early 16th century under the reign of Henry VII's son, King Henry VIII.

King Henry VIII saw Ireland as a potential source of wealth and power for the English Crown, and he wanted to assert his authority and power over its people. Declaring himself king of Ireland, he began the process of establishing colonies in the country. He promoted the Protestant faith in these colonies and sought to suppress the powers of the Gaelic lords who ruled Ireland.

English colonization efforts were peppered with conflicts and resistance from the Irish people, who were violently opposed to England encroaching on their territory. English colonization had a profound impact on Irish history and culture and continues to affect relations between the two countries to this day.

What happened in Ireland would become a prelude to how England would seize, dominate, and colonize territories around the world.

Seven years after Henry VII, Henry VIII's father, came to the throne, America was "discovered." Curious about the New World, King Henry VII decided to fund a voyage of exploration to North America. He would be the first Tudor monarch to do so. The man chosen to lead the expedition was John Cabot.

However, Henry VII did not live long enough to witness the establishment of a colonial settlement in North America. His son, Henry VIII, had very little interest in further exploring the overseas continent.

Nevertheless, the explorations eventually continued, and by the end of the 16th century, the first British colony was established in the Americas. It was named Virginia after Henry VII's granddaughter (Henry VIII's daughter), Queen Elizabeth I, who was known as the "Virgin Queen."

Portrait of Queen Elizabeth I.

John Cabot

Giovanni Caboto, also known as John Cabot, was an Italian explorer. Unlike Christopher Columbus, whose expeditions were backed by the Spanish Crown, Cabot wanted financing and patronage from England.

His efforts paid off when, in the late 15th century, he sailed under the commission of King Henry VII to explore the New World. The hope was that he would discover a westward route to Asia and establish a trade route.

Cabot and his one ship set sail in 1496 from Bristol, but the attempt was soon aborted due to food shortages and bad weather. He tried again the following year, in May 1497, and voyaged across the Atlantic Ocean, eventually reaching North America.

Cabot claimed the land he arrived on for England and aptly named it "New Found Land," which is present-day Newfoundland in Canada.

This would be the first recorded European exploration of the North American mainland since the Vikings first explored the area in 1021. While the voyage was successful, it was also filled with a lot of difficulties, and many crew members died.

Cabot's third and final voyage started in 1498. He left England with five ships and a crew of around three hundred men. To this day, nobody knows exactly what happened to him or his crew. One ship ended up in Ireland, although it was damaged. The other four were never heard from again.

Some believe the ships were lost at sea, while others believe that Cabot made it to the New World and simply stayed there. Historians generally agree he died sometime in 1499 while at sea.

While Cabot did not play a direct role in the colonization of North America, his explorations led to the discovery of another route across the Atlantic Ocean and helped pave the way for future English expeditions undertaken by people like Sir Walter Raleigh and the Virginia Company with the support Queen Elizabeth I.

Portrait of Sir Walter Raleigh.
https://commons.wikimedia.org/wiki/File:Sir_Walter_Ralegh_by_%27H%27_monogrammist.jpg

Spain and Portugal

Although Britain would go on to build the largest empire known to history, Portugal was the first country to start colonizing during the Age of Discovery. In the early 1400s, Portuguese explorers started to look for other places to settle beyond Europe, as well as new trade routes.

Their explorations brought them to North Africa, where they conquered the town of Ceuta in 1415. The islands of Madeira and Cape Verde followed suit.

Portugal's staunch rival, Spain, decided to also start exploring and searching for new land. Christopher Columbus, an Italian explorer, took to the sea in 1492 under the flag of Spain to search for a direct westward route to China and India.

Instead of finding silks and spices, Columbus landed in The Bahamas, establishing the foundation of the Spanish Empire. Portugal and Spain were soon embroiled in a fierce competition for new lands in Asia, Africa, and the Americas.

By 1532, the bulk of the Americas fell under Spanish rule. Portugal, meanwhile, had territories in Africa, Southeast Asia, the Pacific, and the Middle East, with the notable exception of the Philippines, which Spain had already claimed.

With the placement of their colonies, the two countries became the first European nations to establish trading empires, bringing them an influx of wealth.

However, it wasn't long before other European countries, namely France, Germany, the Netherlands, and England, began to expand overseas. These countries began to war against Spain and Portugal to take away land they had already conquered.

The New World quickly became dotted with European colonies.

The Decline of the Spanish Empire

After enjoying several centuries of power and influence, the Spanish Empire began to decline in the 17th century. Despite the wealth that flowed into the country, maintaining colonies and waging wars started to become expensive.

The galleons of gold transported from the Americas were often stolen by pirates or lost at sea in storms or other accidents. To keep the colonies in line or to fight back against revolts, empires had to spend a lot of money maintaining armies and buying weapons.

Wars were often waged in multiple places and dragged on for years. Things were further complicated when enemies joined forces. For example, when the Dutch revolted against Spanish rule, France and

England stepped in to help the Dutch.

When the Dutch eventually won the war, Spain lost many of its territories. The decline of the empire continued with the Anglo-Spanish War and was further exacerbated by a number of revolts within Spain itself when one of the king's advisors, Count-Duke of Olivares, put forward a proposition to raise taxes.

The collapse of the Iberian Union would become the final tipping point in Spain's decline.

The Iberian Union

In 1578, Portugal was at war with Morocco when King Sebastian was killed during the Battle of the Three Kings (also known as the Battle of Alcácer Quibir). His death left the throne of Portugal without an immediate heir. Cardinal Henry, his great-uncle, was appointed king, but he died two years later, plunging the country into a succession crisis.

At this point, the son of Isabella of Portugal and Holy Roman Emperor Charles V, Philip II of Spain, decided to claim the throne in Portugal. He appointed the duke of Alba as the general of the invading army.

Philip II of Spain.
https://commons.wikimedia.org/wiki/File;Jooris_van_der_Straeten_-_Portrait_of_Philip_II_of_Spain.jpg

The battle between the Spanish and the Portuguese forces was short-lived and ended in victory for Spain, with Philip II being crowned king of Portugal.

Following the dynastic crisis and the Battle of Alcântara, the two countries came together under the Iberian Union. In 1580, the two crowns were officially united.

Under this union, the Iberian Peninsula and Spanish and Portuguese overseas possessions were ruled by the Spanish monarchy. However, this was far from an ideal solution for the Portuguese, who didn't like being ruled by the Spanish. By the 17th century, things were becoming complicated for Portugal on several fronts.

By joining together with Spain, Portugal didn't have its own foreign policy, which meant any enemy of Spain became theirs as well. Any wars waged by Spain was a war they had to get involved in. Politically, the influence and power of Portuguese nobles began to decline, with the Spanish increasingly occupying high positions and posts. The increase in taxes by Count-Duke Olivares was the final straw for the Portuguese. They quickly established their own king and aligned themselves with England, one of Spain's biggest enemies.

After around seven decades of being united, Spain was ousted from the Portuguese government, leading to the dissolution of the Iberian Union in 1640. Eventually, Spain had no other choice but to recognize Portugal's independence.

Over time, Portugal was able to regain influence and authority over some of the territories they had lost while Spain's influence continued to decline.

The Protestant Reformation

Prior to the Protestant Reformation, all Christians in western Europe were Roman Catholics. They were led by the pope in Rome.

The Catholic Church was more than just a rich and powerful religious institution. It heavily influenced people's thoughts, actions, and way of life. And people took the church's teachings and values very seriously.

The idea of the Reformation began in 1517 when Martin Luther published his *Ninety-five Theses*.

The *Ninety-five Theses* condemned the Catholic Church's excesses and corrupt behavior, such as asking for payment from people in exchange for the forgiveness of sins. Luther also felt the Bible should be the only spiritual guide for people and rejected the pope's authority over the religion.

The *Ninety-five Theses* was translated from Latin into German, and with the aid of the printing press, it quickly made its way to a wider audience. It didn't take long for large parts of Europe to support Luther's reforms, with countries like Switzerland and Scotland becoming Protestant. However, deeply Catholic countries like Spain supported Rome and the pope. Spain even used the Inquisition to root out Protestants. In short, the continent was soon divided between the two religious beliefs.

The English Reformation

The Reformation made its way to England when King Henry VIII was desperately looking for a way to end his marriage to Catherine of Aragon so he could marry Anne Boleyn.

Catherine had been unable to provide him with a male heir, and he had fallen in love with Anne. However, the pope refused to grant his request for an annulment.

In retaliation, in 1534, Henry decided his authority was above the Catholic Church since his right to rule came directly from God. Parliament passed a law recognizing Henry as the head of the new Church of England and giving him control of the clergy.

Following this, Henry dissolved the English monasteries, took their money, and made the Bible accessible to all.

Henry VIII set Catherine aside and married Anne, though, to her dying day, Catherine considered Henry to be her rightful husband. Anne also failed to produce a male heir and was eventually beheaded. Henry would go on to marry four more times.

Portrait of King Henry VIII.
https://commons.wikimedia.org/wiki/File:1491_Henry_VIII.jpg

After Henry VIII's death, England was torn between Protestantism and Catholicism. When his son Edward became king, the country leaned toward Protestantism, but after his death, when Mary I became queen, Catholicism was enforced. Hundreds of Protestants were persecuted and burned at the stake for their religious views. The persecutions earned Mary the nickname of "Bloody Mary."

The Reformation changed Christianity forever, and today, Protestantism is one of the three main branches of the religion.

The consequences of the Reformation were immediate and long lasting, spawning a number of wars and rebellions, such as the Knights' Revolt in 1522, the German Peasants' War two years later, and the Thirty Years' War. These wars had a significant impact on the British Empire and played an important role in North American history.

In fact, it was one of the primary reasons why Europeans began to leave the continent to settle in North America.

Queen Elizabeth I: Expansion of an Empire

Britain didn't begin to colonize North America immediately following John Cabot's explorations. While Henry VII was intrigued by the New World and the opportunities it could create, his son, Henry VIII, was more preoccupied with domestic affairs. He had little interest in North America. His focus was on strengthening and creating diplomatic ties with other European nations and building a strong British navy.

Elizabeth was crowned queen on November 1ˢᵗ, 1558, following the death of Queen Mary, her half-sister. Her father, King Henry VIII, is best known for having six wives, two of whom were beheaded. His primary reason for marrying multiple times was the lack of a son and heir to the English throne. It's ironic that his daughter, a woman, would go on to reign for forty-five years.

England under the Virgin Queen, as Elizabeth was commonly referred to, witnessed one of the most glorious periods of British history, the Golden Age. During this time, arts and literature thrived. This was the era of Shakespeare, after all. There was peace, stability, and prosperity throughout the country.

This was a sharp contrast to Queen Mary's rule. In the five short years that she reigned, the country was embroiled in a bitter religious fight between Catholics and Protestants. Queen Mary, a Catholic herself, was determined to restore Catholicism to England. Her use of force and violence in the persecution of Protestants earned her the nickname "Bloody Mary." She was viewed as a cold, ruthless, and violent leader. She even had her own sister, Elizabeth, arrested and imprisoned in the Tower of London.

Elizabeth was eventually released, narrowly escaping death. Four years later, she became queen, inheriting a bitterly divided England that had plunged into political and religious turmoil.

Through a blend of cool, ruthless calculation, political acumen, and feminine charms and flattery, Queen Elizabeth became adept at navigating the challenges of being a female ruler. It helped that she was incredibly clever and well educated. Her refusal to marry and subject herself to a man's authority also added to her allure and strength.

During her rule, Britain expanded into Ireland, Wales, and Scotland and began to colonize North America.

The first explorer to be granted permission by the queen was Sir Humphrey Gilbert, who led three expeditions to the Americas with the goal of establishing a colony. All three of his attempts were fruitless. During his final voyage in 1583, his ship was lost at sea.

In 1584, Sir Gilbert's half-brother Walter Raleigh was granted a patent and sailed toward North America.

The Americas

The first permanent British colony in North America was named Jamestown, Virginia, and it was established in 1607. However, it was not the first colony to be founded.

Raleigh tried to establish a colony on Roanoke Island in 1584. The colony was made up of 107 men, but it proved to be a challenge due to the harsh climate and unfamiliar terrain. The effort at maintaining a settlement was abandoned.

A second attempt was made a few years later in July 1587 when 150 colonizers arrived from England, including women and children, under the guidance of John White, who was named governor of the colony.

Soon after arriving, White returned to England to get more supplies. His return was delayed due to Britain's conflict with Spain. When he and Raleigh eventually headed back to Roanoke in 1590, the colony was gone. To this day, nobody knows what happened to the colony or its inhabitants. It is often referred to as the "Lost Colony."

This put a temporary pause on the dream of an English colony in the Americas.

However, Elizabeth's ambition and desire for a colony set the stage for future attempts, and Britain found success when Jamestown was founded. The colonization of America was primarily driven by economic, political, and religious motives.

For many Europeans, the New World was an alluring prospect and a chance to start anew. This was no different for the English, who found the prospect of economic opportunities attractive. Colonization offered the possibility of acquiring land and resources, which, for many, would have been unheard of in England. It allowed the possibility of establishing new trade routes and expanding the market for English goods.

For the English monarchy, colonization was one more way in which it could advance its political ambitions and extend its power and influence across the world. England wanted to challenge the dominance of other European powers like Spain and France, which were already claiming land in the New World.

Many English colonizers were also motivated by religion. In the 17th century, many Europeans who craved religious freedom or feared for their life because of their beliefs began to flee to North America. Feeling threatened in an increasingly hostile religious environment, many chose to escape religious persecution. In the New World, they were free to live and practice as they wished, at least for the most part.

North America slowly became a refuge for all kinds of people and for a myriad of reasons. England was experiencing rapid population growth and suffering from social unrest. In a country that was clearly divided by class, people were eager to find new opportunities. Emigrating to the New World offered them just that: a chance for social advancement and the possibility of starting fresh.

To facilitate the colonization effort, joint-stock companies were established with the help of the English government to provide funding and organizational support. Two of the most famous companies were the Virginia Company and the Massachusetts Bay Company.

Even though England was fairly late to the game of colonizing North America, through a series of strategic moves and victories, it would go on to colonize large swathes of North America.

Chapter 2: Thirteen Colonies and a Revolution

England's First Settlement in the Americas

By the 16th century, England was taking a more aggressive approach to expanding its empire around the world. At home, things were far from ideal, with rising unemployment, food shortages, and religious persecution.

Meanwhile, many European nations were fiercely competing against each other for the acquisition of colonies. Colonies were seen as profitable business ventures and a way of solving the issue of Europe's surplus population.

After the mysterious disappearance of the Roanoke colony in 1590, Jamestown, located in Virginia, became England's second attempt at establishing a settlement. Despite the hardships, this attempt was met with more success.

Jamestown

In December 1606, after the Virginia Company of London (one of the joint-stock companies approved by the English government) funded a trip to North America, over one hundred men and boys sailed from England on three ships. They landed in North America, and by the spring of the following year, they had established a settlement in Virginia called Jamestown, named after King James I.

Jamestown would become the first permanent English colony in North America. It was meant to be a replica of society in England, and English investors were hopeful that this successful settlement would increase their wealth.

The area, located on the banks of the James River, was picked for its location, as the settlement would be bordered by water on three sides and connected to land on another. The water was deep enough for ships to dock and could easily be defended against any attacks by the Spanish.

By the summer of 1607, the inhabitants had built a fort to protect themselves from attacks by local Native Americans. The relationship between the newcomers and the Native Americans was not bad, but it wasn't great either.

On top of this, the early settlers faced a number of challenges, including a harsh and unfamiliar winter. Colonists began to get sick and die from illnesses like fevers, fluxes, and famine. Chief Powhatan and his tribe saved the colonists from complete starvation by sending them gifts of food, and this generosity and kindness saved the settlement from failing.

However, by late 1609, the relationship had soured, and English colonists, scared of being killed by the Powhatans, rarely left their fort and kept to themselves. Times were tough, and the settlers struggled.

By the following year, almost all of the settlers had died because of illness or starvation. They were close to giving up on the settlement entirely when they received word that a fleet carrying Thomas West, 3rd Baron De La Warr, Jamestown's new governor, was on his way.

Things at Jamestown began to turn around after that. In 1612, a man named John Rolfe brought tobacco seeds to the settlement and established a trading relationship with the Powhatans.

The tobacco crops turned Jamestown into a profitable colony and ensured its survival. He married Pocahontas in 1614, which brought peace between the Powhatans and the colonists. The peace lasted until 1622, after which battles and skirmishes broke out between the two groups.

In the meantime, the colony's population continued to increase. Women were recruited from England and shipped to the colony to marry colonists and start families. The colony steadily grew and became a permanent establishment. A legislative assembly was created, which would become the foundation of the present-day United States' representative government.

Tobacco farms were profitable but hard work, so slaves were brought in from Africa to work the land.

Over the next decades, the colonists continued to navigate difficulties, struggles, and battles. In 1699, following a fire that left much of the town destroyed, the government and the people decided to move the capital to Middle Plantation, changing its name to Williamsburg to honor King William III.

Ruins of Jamestown.
https://commons.wikimedia.org/wiki/File:Jamestown_Virginia_ruin.JPG

Williamsburg was a better location and more suited to be the capital of Virginia. Some people continued to live in Jamestown, but it was no longer considered a proper town.

The Thirteen Colonies

By the 18th century, Britain had established twelve additional colonies strategically placed along the Atlantic coast.

The colonies were located and divided into three separate regions, and unsurprisingly, many of them were named after British monarchs like King Charles I and Queen Elizabeth I (the Virgin Queen).

- New England Colonies
  - Connecticut
  - Massachusetts Bay

- o New Hampshire
- o Rhode Island
- Middle Colonies
  - o Delaware
  - o New Jersey
  - o New York
  - o Pennsylvania
- Southern Colonies
  - o Georgia
  - o Maryland
  - o North Carolina
  - o South Carolina
  - o Virginia

The Thirteen Colonies would eventually become the foundation of the modern-day United States.

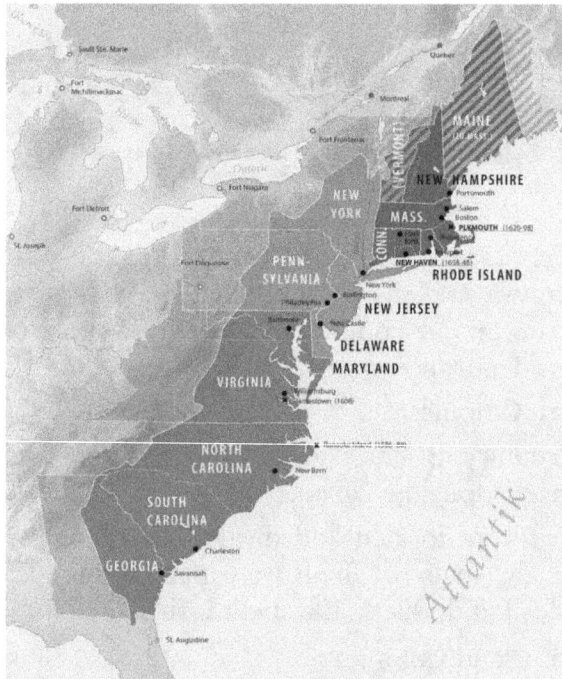

Thirteen Colonies of North America.

Marriage, children, families, and a steady stream of migrants arriving from Britain and continental Europe ensured continued population growth in these North American colonies.

The previously uninhabited wilderness slowly transformed into communities and civilizations. The colonies began to develop their own identity and forged bonds with each other. By the 18th century, the relationship between Britain and its colonies had become tense and strained.

How Britain Controlled North America

Once Britain decided to begin colonizing North America, one of the challenges it faced was how to exert and maintain control over the colonies. Given the geographical distance, this would not be an easy feat; however, Britain managed to do just that by using a combination of economic dominance, military force, and political influence.

The settlements established in the early 1600s, which included Virginia, Massachusetts, and Carolina, helped England exert control over the region. When English settlers arrived, they brought their own culture, language, and institutions with them, which helped to solidify England's presence in the colonies.

Trade was a powerful tool that was used to keep the colonies in line. England dominated the trade networks of the colonies, especially in the 18th century. There was almost nothing the British merchants did not trade.

Everything from sugar and tobacco to cotton, fur, timber, and fish were traded. With the passage of various trade laws, the British government was able to ensure that British merchants maintained their monopoly on trade in North America. The colonists, in turn, were heavily dependent on these merchants to bring them goods.

Life in the colonies was far from ideal, and conflicts and skirmishes between settlements established by other European powers and Native Americans were very common. As a result, it was important for Britain to maintain a strong military presence in the region. These troops helped secure and advance British interests. They also intervened during uprisings or rebellions. The colonists relied on this military force for protection against enemy attacks.

Finally, Britain controlled the colonies through politics. Many of the colonial governors or other political officials received their appointments from the British government; as such, they naturally prioritized British interests and desires over what the colonists preferred or needed.

When we look at the numerous ways in which Britain was entwined with the American colonies and how dependent the colonists were on the motherland, it's easy to understand how the empire managed to have such absolute control.

However, over time, as Britain's demands became increasingly problematic, the colonists began to evaluate their situation and challenge their relationship with Britain.

Over the decades, colonial power and influence grew, as did the size of the colonies. This would end up becoming Britain's downfall, as the colonies eventually began to revolt.

Conflict in the Americas

While moving to the New World provided the colonists with certain freedoms and opportunities, their life was extremely difficult. In the early decades, their survival was dependent on supplies that arrived from Britain or on the kindness of the Native Americans.

When the colonists first arrived, they were faced with the monumental task of building a life out of nothing. They had to clear land, get rid of trees, build shelters and defenses, find a way of growing or catching food, survive in the harsh, unfamiliar climate, and navigate relations with the Native Americans.

Many succumbed to illness or starvation or died in violent clashes with the Native Americans. It was a reality that was difficult to grasp for those living in England.

At first, the relationship between England and the colonies was friendly, amicable, and a necessity. England yielded absolute control over the regions, while the colonists, scrambling to stay alive, were dependent on the empire for food, supplies, and protection against invasion and enemy attacks.

In return, England received enormous benefits from the colonies in the form of valuable resources like precious metals, sugar, and tobacco. These materials were sold to other countries for a steep profit. Wealthy British investors increased their wealth, and the empire got richer.

But while the European powers were busy fighting for new land and grappling over territorial boundaries, the colonists in North America were navigating a new life. They were working against the harsh conditions of their surroundings to create settlements and survive. They began to grow closer and developed a strong sense of unity.

These bonds of nationalism were further deepened during the French and Indian War, which was fought over a period of nine years.

French and Indian War (1754-1763)

This war started in North America and eventually became a theater of the Seven Years' War, a larger global conflict between France and Britain that spanned across several continents. This war will be discussed in greater detail in Chapter 5.

In North America, the dispute began over control of the Upper Ohio River Valley. This strategically located region was claimed by both the French and the British.

The French had established a series of forts in the area, while Britain was looking to expand its own settlements in the region. Tensions continued to rise and eventually escalated into a major armed conflict in 1754 when George Washington led a charge of British forces against the French at Fort Necessity.

During the war, both sides received help, supplies, and reinforcements from their homeland, and it wasn't long before the conflict began to touch other parts of North America, including Canada and various Native American tribes.

Most of the native tribes sided with the French, as they felt they had a better chance of getting their lands back if the French won. The French were less intent on creating permanent settlements and more focused on trading. This was not the case for Britain. The Native Americans saw Britain taking more and more of their land to create settlements. Still, several tribes allied with the British.

British forces under enemy fire.
Internet Archive Book Images, No restrictions, via Wikimedia Commons;
https://commons.wikimedia.org/wiki/File:Indians_ambush_British_at_Battle_of_the_Monongah
ela.jpg

The war came to a head in 1759 when British forces captured the city of Quebec, which was the capital of New France. French resistance largely ended after the British took Montreal in 1760, and the war came to a formal end in 1763 with the signing of the Treaty of Paris.

Although Britain won the war, it came at a steep cost and left the empire in deep debt. The war also changed the balance of power in North America, with Britain emerging as the clear power.

For the colonists, the win was a huge boost and contributed to feelings of nationalism and patriotism. For them, the war had little to do with warring empires and everything to do with their ability to band together and vanquish a common enemy. It made them realize their own strengths and abilities and wonder if they could be more than just a group of separate colonies.

Repercussions of the War for Britain

The Seven Years' War cost the British dearly. In a bid to recoup the expenses and raise money for the army, the British Parliament turned to the colonies. After all, the French and Indian War had been waged to protect the colonies from French incursions.

Four acts were quickly passed, starting with the Sugar Act of 1764. Under this act, any sugar or molasses that was imported into the colonies from foreign sugar-producing islands was subject to a tax. They implemented the tax knowing that Boston and the New England colonies relied heavily on these items to make rum, which they exported to other regions, such as West Africa. In West Africa, rum was often used as a way of purchasing slaves.

Because rum was such a significant source of revenue for the colonies, additional taxes cut into the profits. Rather than paying the tax, many colonists began to look elsewhere for these goods.

The Stamp Act was passed a year later, imposing taxes on every kind of printed material that required an embossed stamp, including pamphlets and playing cards. People began to voice their unhappiness and protested against these taxes.

Undeterred, Britain passed the Townshend Acts in 1767 and 1768. This time, taxes were placed on items like glass, tea, and paper that were imported from Britain. The colonists were incensed and began to protest in earnest. Things got worse when British troops arrived from England to enforce the acts.

Boston Massacre – 1770

A series of events, starting with the Boston Massacre, fueled the growing sentiment for independence. The Boston Massacre, considered to be a pivotal event in American history, took place on March 5th, 1770, when some colonists started to taunt a group of British soldiers stationed outside the Customs House in Boston.

The soldiers felt threatened and eventually started to fire on the unarmed colonists. Three colonists died, and two more died later from their wounds.

Bostonians and the colonists in general were incensed by the massacre, and demand for American independence grew after the incident. The British soldiers were later tried for the killings. The colonists sought to give them a fair trial; two of them were found guilty of manslaughter, but the other six soldiers were acquitted.

For the colonists, the Boston Massacre became further proof of British oppression and helped to stoke the revolutionary spirit.

Boston Tea Party – 1773

Another key event that united the colonies in their resistance against the British and helped to spark the American Revolution was the Boston Tea Party.

In addition to the series of acts passed between 1764 and 1768, the British government decided to pass the Tea Act in 1773. Under this act, the British East India Company was given a monopoly on tea sales in the colonies.

Angry at the British government for imposing taxes on the colonies without giving them proper representation or caring about their issues, a group of protestors decided to take action. Later in the year, on December 16th, a group of colonists disguised themselves as Native Americans and boarded three British ships.

Once the colonists were on the ships, they dumped over three hundred chests of tea imported by the East India Company into the Atlantic Ocean.

1846 lithograph by Nathaniel Currier depicting the Boston Tea Party.
https://commons.wikimedia.org/wiki/File:Boston_Tea_Party_Currier_colored.jpg

When the British Parliament found out, they were furious, and the ramifications for this insolent behavior came swiftly in the form of a series of acts known as the Coercive or Intolerable Acts.

These harsh measures were meant to be a punishment for the colonists' rebellious behavior and get them "back in line."

The Intolerable Acts

Feeling that the colonies were getting out of hand, Britain decided it needed to take drastic steps to assert its authority.

The Coercive or Intolerable Acts came quickly on the heels of the Boston Tea Party. They were passed by the British Parliament in 1774. They are as follows:

1) The Boston Port Act – This act closed the port of Boston until the colonists paid for all the tea that had been destroyed during the Boston Tea Party. This was designed to cripple them financially, as ships could no longer go in and out of the port to conduct trade.

2) The Massachusetts Government Act – This reduced the power of the colonial government in Massachusetts and placed it under British control. This would make it even harder for Bostonians to have a say in politics.

3) The Administration of Justice Act – Under this act, British officials who were accused of committing a crime in the colonies were to be tried in Britain instead of where the crime took place. This was a slap in the face for the colonists because they knew these crimes would rarely be punished in Britain and that they had set a precedent for conducting fair trials. It was another way for Britain to oppress them and take away their control.

4) The Quartering Act – This act required that housing and supplies for British troops be provided by the colonists. The same troops that had been sent to enforce acts and make sure colonists didn't step out of line would now have to be maintained by them!

However, the acts did not have the effect Britain desired. The Intolerable Acts left the colonists outraged and united in their hatred toward British rule. The conditions were finally ripe enough for a revolt, and the storm that had been brewing for years came to a head, sparking the American Revolution.

The American Revolution

America's fight for independence began with the Battles of Lexington and Concord in April 1775 when colonial troops clashed with British troops.

Several months later, in July, the Continental Congress, which represented the Thirteen Colonies, issued the Declaration of Causes and Necessity of Taking Up Arms. This essentially declared that the colonies were taking up arms to fight for their rights as British subjects.

The Continental Congress adopted the Declaration of Independence in 1776, officially severing the colonies' ties with Britain. They declared the United States to be a sovereign nation.

However, the American Revolutionary War did not end there. It continued for several more years, with dozens of battles fought throughout the colonies. The war eventually wound to a close with a victory for the Americans.

1781 Siege of Yorktown – The British surrender.
https://commons.wikimedia.org/wiki/File:John_Trumbull_-
The_Surrender_of_Lord_Cornwallis_at_Yorktown,_October_19,_1781_-_1832.4_-
Yale_University_Art_Gallery.jpg

The fighting came to an end in 1783 with the signing of the Treaty of Paris. Under the terms of the treaty, the United States was recognized as an independent nation, and the country's boundaries were formally established.

America's revolution became an inspiration for many other revolutionary movements, including the French Revolution. It also established America's reputation as a democratic nation founded on the principles of liberty, equality, and self-government. The colonists had taken on the greatest empire in the world and won! For Britain, the loss of the Thirteen Colonies was utterly devastating.

Impact of the Revolution on Britain

Despite the initial struggles of establishing settlements, over time, the colonies began to thrive. At the time of the revolution, the Thirteen Colonies were an invaluable source of raw materials and created a significant market for British goods.

The loss of the colonies meant a sharp decline in the empire's wealth and influence. For Britain, the defeat at the hands of the colonies was humiliating and a blow to its prestige and reputation as a colonial power. The revolt against them was seen as a challenge to Britain's authority, and it sparked other anti-colonial movements. Countries began to think that if America could do it, why couldn't they?

The war also left Britain crippled financially. It had been an expensive undertaking, and the government had been forced to borrow large amounts of money to fund the war. This further burdened an already significant national debt. Britain paid a heavy price in human lives too, losing a lot of soldiers in the colonies.

However, losing the colonies did not lead to a severing of ties. Britain still had other colonies in the region, and a mutual desire for economic prosperity ensured trade continued between the two countries.

Chapter 3: Trade and the Slave Trade

Maritime Control

From the earliest days of civilization, it was an accepted fact that whoever controlled the seas could exert some form of control over the nations bordering them.

Today, when we think of "naval power," we automatically think of Great Britain, an island that, at one point in time, controlled over 25 percent of the world. Because of its geographic location, Britain has always relied on the sea for trading, exploring, and defending. Britain's navy has also played a crucial role in expanding and protecting the empire's interests at home and abroad.

This same naval power helped fight battles during the Napoleonic Wars and win two world wars.

When the Seven Years' War ended in a British victory, Britain emerged as a powerful maritime force. The empire's power and influence became undisputable, and in the 18th and 19th centuries, the empire had absolute control of the world's oceans.

Maritime power not only helped the empire expand, but it also helped Britain become a very wealthy nation, as the trade routes provided access to valuable resources and markets around the world. At home, building ships and port industries provided a source of employment and helped with economic growth.

Britain's Navy

The British Royal Navy is one of the oldest and one of the most respected naval forces in the world. Its inception dates back to the mid-16th century.

As Britain's influence grew, so did the navy's role. During Britain's colonization period, the navy played an integral part in projecting the country's power around the world and shaping the course of history.

During the 18th and 19th centuries, Britain was the largest empire in the world, and its navy was the most powerful. During the French Revolution and the Napoleonic Wars, the Royal Navy was at its most efficient, and it commanded the seas. Under skillful command, it was able to successfully defend against French and Spanish attacks.

The Royal Navy also played a big role in the exploration of the world, as explorers headed out to discover the Northwest Passage or Terra Australis. The voyages and the discoveries that were made contributed greatly to people's knowledge of the world.

Today, the Royal Navy may not yield quite the same power as it used to, but it remains highly respected, and its legacy continues to shape Britain's national identity.

The Transatlantic Slave Trade

While the Royal Navy can be admired for many things, its legacy does have a darker, more shameful side.

Slavery, which was essentially a system of forcibly transporting and trafficking humans from Africa to the Americas and elsewhere, played a crucial role in the expansion of the British Empire. The process was facilitated by the British navy.

The first English slaving expedition took place in 1562 when John Hawkins sailed from England to Africa. He captured over three hundred Africans and sold them to Spanish colonists in the Americas. By the 17th century, the slave trade had become a thriving business for the English.

How did it work? The transatlantic slave trade was a route shaped almost like a triangle that went from Europe to Africa, from Africa to the Americas, and then from the Americas to Europe.

While traveling this route, merchants exported goods to Africa; in exchange, they received spices, precious materials like gold or ivory, and, of course, enslaved Africans. The ships containing all these "goods" made their way to the colonies in the Americas, primarily the North

American colonies and the Caribbean.

The colonists purchased African slaves from the merchants for tobacco, cotton, sugar, and other items. The slaves were then sold to those who could afford them.

The inspection of a slave.
https://commons.wikimedia.org/wiki/File:The_inspection_and_sale_of_a_slave.jpg

The purchased slaves worked in the household, on plantations, or in mines. In the meantime, British merchants took the American goods back to Europe and sold them for a profit.

It was a thriving business that enriched investors, individuals, and empires. Even though Britain was one of several other European powers involved in the slave trade, it was one of the most successful.

As Britain embraced its role as a maritime power, the navy's power and influence also grew, and it became increasingly involved in the slave trade. The navy's ships were used to protect British slave ships from attacks by pirates or other enemies, and they were also used to attack slave ships that were owned by other empires and countries.

Roughly 70 percent of all enslaved Africans were transported to the Americas by Britain and Portugal.

Britain was most active in the trade between 1640 and 1807. Historians estimate that around 3.1 million Africans were trafficked, with around 2.7 million surviving the journey and going on to be sold to British colonies.

While the navy's role made the slave trade more efficient, it would go on to play a key role in the abolition of slavery. The navy patrolled the seas and intercepted slave ships to prevent the transportation of enslaved Africans.

It would be impossible to summarize the value of Britain's navy in just a few short paragraphs. However, it can still be clearly seen that Britain's navy was closely intertwined with the transatlantic slave trade, from the earliest days of colonization to slavery's eventual abolition in the 19th century.

Economic Benefits of Slavery

The exploitation of millions of people is a deeply repugnant concept, and it's hard to imagine that entire nations would willingly participate in such an unethical practice. However, people did.

But why? Well, it brought immense wealth to the participating countries, such as Britain, Portugal, Spain, France, and even the Netherlands. Enslaved Africans were forced to work on fields and farms and cultivate crops like tobacco, sugar, cotton, and coffee. These items were in high demand in Europe and the Americas and generated huge incomes. And it didn't just end there.

The profits from the slave trade were used to fund the growth of industries, such as textiles. The finances, in turn, were used to expand colonial empires. It was a vicious, endless cycle where Africans were victimized over and over again.

Globally, the slave trade helped to create an economic system that facilitated the exchange of goods and services between different parts of the world. This system, reprehensible though it was, provided a foundation for the growth of modern-day capitalism and international trade.

But all of this wealth and riches came at an immense cost, one paid dearly by enslaved Africans who were treated as less than human.

Treatment of Slaves

Merchant Ships

Slaves were captured by slave traders, usually along the west coast of Africa. They did so by raiding villages at night. They captured men, women, children, and entire families and whisked them into waiting slave ships.

Goods like guns, alcohol, and textiles were also traded with African traders for slaves. These traders captured or bought slaves from other tribes to sell them to Europeans. Another way was through debt bondage. Traders provided loans to African leaders and chiefs, using slaves as collateral. When the loans went unpaid, the slaves were claimed as payment.

Once captured, slaves were taken to a holding area before being transported to the Americas or another colony on slave ships. The conditions on these ships were brutal and inhumane. Slave traders saw Africans as nothing more than property, so basic human rights and dignity were denied to them.

The slave ships crossed the Atlantic in a journey that is known as the Middle Passage. The voyage took several months.

Treated like cargo rather than human beings, Africans were usually shackled together and packed tightly into confined spaces for the entire duration of the journey, usually in the ship's hold.

The ship's hold was located below the main deck and was a dark and cramped space. It was not designed as a living space and lacked the necessary ventilation, lighting, or even a bathroom.

Packed together like sardines, unable to move around, Africans had no choice but to relieve themselves on the spot. They were forced to live in their own waste, and many succumbed to disease and illness, dying before they ever reached their final destination.

Painting of a slave ship by Johann Rugendas, a German painter who saw this scene with his own eyes.
https://commons.wikimedia.org/wiki/File:Navio_negreiro_-_Rugendas_1830.jpg

Africans also endured extreme temperatures, poor nutrition, and brutality from the ship's crews. They were beaten and tortured, and women and children were sexually assaulted and/or abused.

An African's survival often depended entirely on how humane the ship's captain or crew decided to be. Some ships had a higher mortality rate than others.

Working Conditions

For those who managed to survive the voyage, the working conditions they faced in the colonies were no better.

On plantations and farms, slaves usually worked from sunrise to sunset with few breaks. Days off were a luxury and not easily awarded. Slaves were treated with harsh brutality.

Some common tasks for the enslaved people on sugar plantations included clearing land, planting and cultivating crops, and harvesting and processing the sugarcane. The work was not only physically demanding, but it was also quite dangerous since it required the use of heavy machinery or tools like machetes.

The weather added another layer of brutality, with workers exposed to extreme heat and forced to endure the beating sun, heavy rains, or cold. And when they got sick, they still had to work. It was not uncommon for slaves to die of exhaustion, dehydration, or malnourishment.

Tea plantations had similar working conditions and involved a labor-intensive process of planting, pruning, plucking, and processing the tea leaves. Workers were paid little to nothing for their work. Their living conditions were no better, with cramped, overcrowded housing and limited access to food, healthcare, and education the norm.

Tobacco was also a hot commodity and a major cash crop. The working conditions on these farms were similar to what slaves on tea and sugar plantations endured. They worked from dawn to dusk and were typically given off one day a week, but this was spent on other chores or tasks for the owner.

Psychologically, enslaved people were subjected to significant trauma and emotional abuse. Physically, they were beaten, raped, or subjected to other brutal punishments for the smallest infraction. Families were often torn apart and sold to others. The living conditions were also poor and inadequate.

Of course, there were exceptions. Not every family or owner treated their slaves in such a manner. There are stories of kindness and compassion, and some slaves lived a far nicer life than others. However, that doesn't take away from the fact that they were still slaves.

East India Company

In 1600, a group of English merchants with a royal charter from Queen Elizabeth I established the East India Company. The East India Company was a trading company with the goal of facilitating trade with countries in East Asia, specifically India, Indonesia, and China.

Operating out of Asia, the East India Company was granted a monopoly on English trade with the East Indies. The company used its power to build an extensive trading network throughout Asia, trading in a wide range of goods.

Hot commodities included textiles, spices, opium, and tea. Over time, the company grew and expanded its trading activities and soon became the dominant player in the Indian subcontinent. By the 18th century, the East India Company had become political and began to be used as an agent of British imperialism.

The East India Company would go on to control large parts of India, Bangladesh, and Pakistan. To maintain its monopoly over the region, they established the East India Company Army. This private army engaged in military campaigns, secured the company's interests in India, and played an enormous role in the colonization and subjugation of the region.

It wasn't long before the company began to use its military might to impose British will on local rulers and extract resources from these regions. The East India Company essentially became the ruler of these areas.

A continued lack of resources led to widespread poverty and famine and stunted the development of these Asian countries in numerous ways. The effects of Britain's actions during this period continue to impact many developing countries to this day.

Tensions between the British and Indian people began to rise, eventually culminating in the Indian Rebellion of 1857, also known as the Indian Mutiny.

This eventually led to the end of East India Company's absolute control in India. However, the British government moved in and took direct control of the region.

Sugar and Tea

Tea and the daily ritual of sitting down for it several times throughout the day are so quintessentially British and rooted so deeply in British culture that it's hard to remember that they didn't always exist in the country.

While tea had existed for centuries in China, the English wouldn't hear about it until the mid-1600s.

Prior to tea arriving in the country, most English people drank coffee. In the 1650s, Dutch traders began to bring tea to Europe. Initially, this delicious exotic drink, referred to as "China drink" by English diarist Samuel Pepys, was seen as a novelty and not accessible to many.

As the story goes, tea began to gain popularity in England after King Charles II married the king of Portugal's daughter, Catherine of Braganza. Tea was a popular drink for the Portuguese aristocrats, and the new queen of England was used to drinking it regularly. When she got married, she arrived in England with several ships full of luxury items from Portugal. Among them was a chest of tea.

It didn't take long for British nobles and aristocrats to take up the practice. By 1664, England was importing its own tea, but high taxes made it a very expensive drink that only the wealthy could afford. Therefore, tea was seen as a mark of luxury and wealth.

But over time, everyone wanted some. In fact, demand was so high that smuggling tea became a lucrative enterprise. However, it continued to be expensive and not accessible to all.

When William Pitt the Younger became prime minister in 1783, he dramatically reduced the tea tax from almost 120 percent to a mere 12.5 percent. Smugglers gave up their operations, and tea became affordable for all backgrounds and classes.

Tea took Britain by storm, and absolutely everyone wanted it. Eventually, milk began to be added to tea either to cool it down so it wasn't so hot or to add flavor.

Tea and sugar soon became the focal points of British trade and import, with slavery playing an integral role in their trade and production.

Hot Commodities and the Transatlantic Slave Trade

After tea and sugar were introduced to the European markets, everyone wanted some. However, the production was extremely labor intensive and required a large amount of land and resources. It was also important for the merchants to keep costs down so they could have bigger profits.

To meet the increasing demands of the population, colonial powers in Europe established plantations in places like India, North America, and the Caribbean. Enslaved Africans were brought to these regions to work on the plantations and cultivate and harvest tea, sugar, and other produce. And best of all, it was mostly free labor.

Enslaved labor was particularly prevalent in the Caribbean, where sugar plantations were the largest and most profitable enterprises. For tea production, Sri Lanka and India had the biggest plantations.

Chapter 4: The Empire "Down Under"

As the British Empire was firmly in control of the seas, it stands to reason that Britain would continue its explorations by sea.

Having conquered parts of North America, Africa, and Asia, Britain set its sights on the largely undiscovered Southern Hemisphere, or the world "down under."

To help them with their explorations, the British government enlisted the help of English explorer and navigator James Cook.

James Cook and Terra Australis

James Cook was best known for his voyages in the Pacific Ocean and his significant contributions to mapping Terra Australis.

Captain Cook's first voyage started in 1768. He had two goals. One was to observe the transit of Venus from Tahiti, and the other was to explore the Pacific region and look for the southern continent that Greek philosophers and scholars were convinced existed.

This southern continent was referred to as Terra Australis Incognita or "Great Unknown Land." It was a hypothetical continent that some philosophers, including Aristotle and Pythagoras, thought was out there. They felt certain that given the shape of the earth (a perfect sphere) and the distribution of land, a landmass had to exist in the Southern Hemisphere to balance out the weight of the north. Medieval European scholars also believed in this theory, and they continued to promote the idea of Terra Australis.

By the 18th century, European explorers, some of whom had circumnavigated the globe, believed they had disproved the theory of Terra Australis. Explorers had been unable to locate a large landmass in the Southern Hemisphere; what they had discovered instead was a lot of water and smaller islands.

Even though Terra Australis was ultimately discovered to not exist, the idea that it could had a significant impact on world exploration, cartography, and theories around the shape and structure of earth.

When James Cook set out, he hoped to find Terra Australis. However, when he sailed south from Tahiti, he made several landings on the islands of New Zealand and eastern Australia.

HMS Resolution and Discovery in Tahiti
https://commons.wikimedia.org/wiki/File;John_Cleveley_the_Younger,_Views_of_the_South_Se
as_(No._3_of_4).jpg

In 1770, Cook claimed possession of the east coast of Australia for Britain and named it New South Wales. He made contact with the Indigenous people of Australia, becoming the first European to do so.

Cook's second voyage began a few years later, in 1772. He sailed farther south than previous explorers and ended up reaching the Antarctic Circle. His explorations resulted in extensive observations of the region's geography, the weather, animals, and plants. His work provided the most accurate understanding of the Southern Hemisphere at that time and enabled further explorations of the area.

Cook undertook one more voyage in 1776, which led him to the Pacific Northwest of North America and to the Hawaiian Islands. Cook died in Hawaii in 1779 after a violent encounter with some locals.

Indigenous Australians

The Indigenous population of Australia is the Aboriginal and Torres Strait Islanders. They were the first inhabitants of Australia and its surrounding islands.

Before the European settlers started to arrive on the island in 1788, approximately three hundred to one thousand Indigenous tribes were settled across the continent. Each tribe had its own unique culture, traditions, and language, with their rich cultural heritage dating back to more than sixty thousand years.

They lived off of the land using traditional practices like hunting, gathering, and farming. Their ways of living and their social harmony were disrupted by the arrival of the European settlers, which had devastating impacts.

As the Europeans had done in the Americas, they began to take away land from the Indigenous population as they began to build settlements. Chaos, widespread violence, and the spread of disease followed.

Colonization of Australia

Australia started to be colonized by Great Britain in the late 18th century, nearly two decades after Cook first claimed New South Wales for the empire.

At that time, Britain was dealing with overcrowding in its prisons, and the government didn't know what to do with all the convicts. The British were also looking to expand their territories overseas to continue supporting the country's economic interests.

A decision was made by the government to establish a penal colony on the continent of Australia. British ships carrying soldiers and convicts soon started to set sail to the southern landmass.

On January 26th, 1788, the first fleet of ships landed in Sydney Cove. Governor Arthur Phillip oversaw the settlement of this first colony, which was called the Colony of New South Wales.

The early years of the colony were marked by growing pains and harsh conditions. Like the American colonists before them, the new settlers of New South Wales faced a number of challenges and difficulties, such as illnesses, food shortages, and conflicts with the Indigenous Australians.

However, they persevered, and with support from Britain, the colony continued to grow. Eventually, other settlements along the coast were established. The British were there to stay.

Very quickly, the colonizers ousted (often forcibly) Indigenous tribes and nations from their lands, claimed ownership of their resources, and began to impose their own laws, culture, and traditions on the native population.

Even though the settlements were expanding, the economy was struggling. This changed when gold was discovered in Victoria in 1851. The discovery led to thousands of immigrants from around the world madly dashing to Australia, hoping to make their fortune. This massive influx of people and investment helped Britain grow Australia's economy.

Entrepreneurs from Britain seized the rush as a perfect opportunity to establish businesses, while banks and other investors financed the development of the mining industry along with other sectors of the economy.

Soon, politics became significant. A growing population needed greater political representation and a democratic government. In 1851, Victoria became a separate colony, and a responsible government was adopted in 1855. For the first time, the parliament, modeled largely on the British system, was elected by the people instead of the British government. The colonies spanning across Australia soon had democratic systems in place that were separate from the British.

The gold rush was significant in the colonization of Australia because it's what gave Britain the power to shape the continent's economic and political growth, which, in turn, contributed to its own growth as an empire.

But through this process, the British were not kind. Indigenous people faced cultural genocide and dispossession. They had to give up their identity and way of life to pave the way for British settlers. The legacy of their actions continues to impact the Indigenous Australians to this day.

Penal Colony

The first eleven ships full of convicts arrived at Sydney Cove in late January 1788. Under the command of Captain Arthur Phillip, the ships were known as the First Fleet. The convicts were mostly poor men and women who had committed minor or petty crimes like fraud or theft.

Lithograph of the First Fleet arriving in Australia.
https://commons.wikimedia.org/wiki/File:The_First_Fleet_entering_Port_Jackson,_January_26,_1788,_drawn_1888_A9333001h.jpg

Their arrival caused immediate tensions with the Aboriginals in the Sydney area. The Eora people did not want strangers encroaching on their territory, and many conflicts ensued over food, land, and resources.

Europeans also brought with them a number of illnesses, like smallpox, which were foreign to the Eora. Thousands of them died from diseases.

Over the span of around a century, more than 150,000 convicted criminals were brought from Britain to Australia.

These convicts weren't just sitting around in prison cells. They were quickly put to work building much of the early infrastructure of the colony. They built roads, public buildings, houses, bridges, and much else.

Once their sentences were over, most convicts decided to remain in Australia and build a new life for themselves. Over time, many convicts rose above the stigma of being criminals and became successful and well-known settlers, playing a significant role in the development of Australian society.

Today, Australia is a developed, first-world, democratic nation with a population of well over twenty-five million people. However, its history as a penal colony left an imprint on its national identity and, in the past, has caused friction with England.

Second British Empire

The "Second British Empire" is a term that is often used to refer to the period of British imperial expansion between the late 19th and early 20th centuries. During this period, the British Empire was at its largest, with an empire that stretched from one end of the world to the other.

The period was characterized by a focus on formal colonization and territorial control and differed from the earlier era when British imperialism was more focused on trade and informal influence. In short, Britain was clear, open, and aggressive about its imperial goals.

There were a few reasons for this shift. One of them was increasing competition from other European powers. The British desired to secure more and more resources and markets. They were fueled by greed and also held the absolute belief that they were better than everyone else.

To have built the kind of empire they did and to yield the control they did, Britain had to believe in its own superiority. The British enforced their culture, religion, civilization, and language on the world because they believed it was the best.

The empire's expansion at this time happened through a combination of military conquest, economic exploitation, and diplomacy. Colonial administrations were established by the British government in many territories, and these administrations often imposed the British way on the local population.

Some historians believe the colonization of Australia was viewed as a fresh start for Britain, especially on the heels of losing the Americas. They had lost an entire continent and were now striving to gain another one. In some ways, Britain was fairly successful, as Australia remained a British colony for over a century and only gained their independence in 1901. However, Australia was not nearly as lucrative as the Americas had been in terms of wealth, trade, or vastness of resources.

In other words, Australia was important to Britain, but it could never replace the loss of the Americas.

The Decline of the Second British Empire

Around the mid-20th century, the power and influence of the British Empire began to decline, as more and more countries called for independence. The notion of self-determination gained momentum in many European colonies.

By this time, the United States had become a force of its own, so it was hard not to make comparisons. More countries wanted to be like the US, free from the shackles and control of a foreign empire.

The process of decolonization reached a fevered pitch after the Second World War, with most of the British colonies gaining their independence by the 1960s.

The sun was starting to set on the British Empire.

Chapter 5: The French Issue

England and France – Battle of Two Empires

Today, France and England enjoy a good and dependable relationship. They are friends and allies who share similar values and policies, and they have supported each other through numerous wars and conflicts, the most significant one being when England declared war on Germany after Hitler invaded France. The Allies worked together to liberate France from Nazi occupation.

However, this wasn't always the case. The two empires have a long and complicated history where they often flip-flopped between periods of friendship and cooperation and hostility and conflict.

Throughout the Middle Ages and into the early modern period, the two nations mostly saw each other as staunch enemies and were constantly at war with each other. They were fierce rivals competing for territories, influence, and global power.

One of the most famous wars between the two countries was the Hundred Years' War, which actually lasted over one hundred years. This war was a series of ongoing conflicts that took place from 1337 to 1453. The original conflict began when King Edward III of England and King Philip VI of France claimed to be the rightful heir to the French throne.

This dispute over who had the claim to the French throne and ongoing territorial disputes added to the tensions and eventually spiraled into a war that lasted for over a century.

After the French won the Battle of Castillon on October 9th, 1453, the war finally came to an end, along with England's rule in France. England lost its possessions on the continent except for the port of Calais, which remained under English control for two hundred years until its recapture by the French in 1558.

The end of the Hundred Years' War ushered in a period of relative stability between the two nations.

Collage of paintings depicting the Hundred Years' War.
Blaue Max, CC BY-SA 4.0 <https://creativecommons.org/licenses/by-sa/4.0>, via Wikimedia Commons; https://commons.wikimedia.org/wiki/File:Hundred_years_war_collage.jpg

The Seven Years' War

The Seven Years' War was the first true global conflict the world had seen, as it involved most of the major European powers and their respective colonies. It began in 1756 and ended in 1763. The main point of contention was the competing interests of the major powers in North America, Europe, and India.

The conflict had actually begun two years earlier in North America when France and England started arguing over who had control of the Ohio River Valley. Within a couple of years, the war spilled over to Europe.

France, Russia (at least until 1762), Austria, and Sweden banded together to form an alliance known as the Family Compact against Britain and Prussia, who had their own alliance.

Battle of Quebec

The Battle of Quebec, also known as the Battle of the Plains of Abraham, is considered to be one of the most important conflicts of the Seven Years' War. The decisive British win put an end to France's plans for expansion in Canada.

The battle started badly for France. Although French defenders were stationed on the Plains of Abraham outside of Quebec City, they were surprised by an attack from British forces led by General James Wolfe. French forces outnumbered the British, but the element of surprise caught them completely off-guard, and they were unable to mount an effective defense.

After a three-month siege by British forces, the battle eventually started on September 13th, 1759 and lasted for approximately one hour. It was short but brutal, with both sides suffering heavy casualties. General Wolfe himself was fatally injured.

The Death of General Wolfe *by Benjamin West.*
https://commons.wikimedia.org/wiki/File:Benjamin_West_005.jpg

Despite this loss, the British managed to hold their position and gain control of the city.

The following spring, France made an attempt to recapture Quebec. The French successfully forced the British to retreat, but it wasn't a lasting success. France's attempt ended in a victory for Britain, and the French surrendered the city. With this surrender, French rule officially ended in Canada.

The battle was significant because it was seen as a turning point in the war. It gave Britain control of Canada, which had previously been mainly under French control. By losing the battle, France's influence in North America decreased dramatically while giving Britain dominance over global affairs.

Battle of Rossbach

The Battle of Rossbach was another significant battle in the war. It was fought between Prussia and France on November 5th, 1757.

While the French were trying to coordinate an attack on Berlin, the capital of Prussia, they were intercepted by King Frederick II and his Prussian army.

The extremely well-trained and disciplined Prussian forces outnumbered the French by almost two to one, winning a swift and decisive victory. This gave them an important strategic advantage and prevented an attack on Berlin, which would have been a major blow to the war effort.

The battle also established King Frederick as one of the greatest military commanders of his time and put Prussia on the map as a major power in Europe. The victory at Rossbach contributed to Britain eventually winning the Seven Years' War.

Treaty of Paris

When it became clear that France was losing the Seven Years' War, France began to negotiate for peace. The war finally came to an end in 1763 with the signing of the Treaty of Paris. The conditions of the treaty had significant political and economic consequences for the empires and their colonies, shifting the balance of power in Europe.

Under the terms of the treaty, France had to cede most of its North American territories, including Canada, to Britain. The Caribbean island of Grenada and the Indian port of Pondicherry were also handed over to Britain, marking the beginning of Britain's dominance in India.

Spain, which entered the war in 1761 to help France, had to cede Florida to Great Britain. In exchange, they got back Havana, Cuba, and Manila in the Philippines.

With the signing of the treaty, France's colonial aspirations in North America came to an end and firmly established Britain as the dominant European power on the continent. Britain gained control over key trading routes and territories, which played a big role in fueling its economic growth and influence over the next century.

As we saw above, the treaty also marked the beginning of tensions between Britain and its North American colonies. These tensions would eventually lead to the American Revolution a few years later.

Napoleon Bonaparte

No book on the British Empire would be complete without discussing Napoleon Bonaparte, a French military and political leader who rose to prominence during the French Revolution and eventually became the emperor of France.

Born to a poor but noble family on the island of Corsica, Napoleon was educated in France. After graduating from the French military academy in 1785, he started his military career in the French Army. The French Revolution started soon after, in 1789. During this time, he rose quickly through the ranks, going from second lieutenant to brigadier general by the age of twenty-four.

Portrait of Napoleon at twenty-three by Henri Félix Emmanuel Philippoteaux.
https://commons.wikimedia.org/wiki/File:Napoleon_-_2.jpg

Napoleon's exceptional leadership skills and strategic thinking made him the perfect choice to lead the French Army. However, in 1799, he shocked the country by seizing power, and he would go on to crown himself as emperor of France in 1804.

Using his brilliant military skills, Napoleon greatly expanded the French Empire by waging wars against other European nations and coalitions. His power and influence began to decline in 1812 after his failed invasion of Russia. In 1814, he was forced to abdicate the throne and went to Elba, where he lived in exile.

The following year, he returned to power, but it was short-lived. After a devastating defeat at the Battle of Waterloo, Napoleon left politics for good. He lived the rest of his life in exile on the island of St. Helena until his death at the age of fifty-one.

Napoleon and Britain

A fierce French nationalist, Napoleon's relationship with Britain was complicated, with the nation eventually becoming his greatest enemy.

In the beginning, Napoleon had respect and admiration for many aspects of Britain's society, such as its education and legal system. But as his own ambitions for France began to grow, so did his resentment toward Britain, which was a major naval power.

Napoleon found himself increasingly butting heads with Britain, whose power and influence kept getting in the way of his own expansionist policies. Britain had more colonies, more resources, and more money, so it was in a strong position to challenge France.

Britain was also allied with many European powers, powers that opposed Napoleon's ambitions. Britain's blockade of French ports during the Napoleonic Wars was a point of contention. The blockade had a severe impact on France's economy, leading to food shortages and high inflation. And every battle that Napoleon lost to Britain chipped away at his honor and prestige, and he took it as a personal insult.

Little by little, his feelings of bitterness toward Britain increased until the country became a bitter enemy.

Napoleonic Wars

The Napoleonic Wars (named after Napoleon) were a series of battles and conflicts waged between 1803 and 1815. They were fought between France and several other European powers, including Great Britain.

Much like the Seven Years' War, the battles took place all over the world and were spread out over numerous continents, although most of the fighting happened in Europe. The main players in the Napoleonic Wars were Great Britain, France, Austria, Prussia, Russia, and Spain.

The wars initially started to maintain France's strength and position within Europe, but they soon spiraled into a power trip for Napoleon, who wanted to dominate the continent.

France very briefly held the title of most influential power in Europe, but it was short-lived.

As part of Napoleon's plan to dominate all of Europe, he established puppet states, crowned himself king of Italy, and made his brothers kings in neighboring nations.

People soon began to turn against France, whom they viewed as an outside power, and their occupation under its rule.

At first, Napoleon and his military campaigns seemed indestructible, as the military genius won victory after victory, but the tide eventually turned, and his fortunes dramatically declined. A few of the most significant battles of the Napoleonic Wars include the following:

1) **Battle of Marengo** – This battle was fought on June 14th, 1800, between French and Austrian troops near the city of Alessandria, Italy. The battle was chaotic, and both sides suffered a lot of casualties. However, the French Army managed to break through the Austrian lines and send them back. The French won the battle and secured control of northern Italy. This battle helped to establish France as a dominant power in Italy and cleared the way for French expansion across Europe.

2) **Battle of Trafalgar** – This was a critical naval engagement fought between the British Royal Navy and the French and Spanish fleets. It took place off the southwest coast of Spain on October 21st, 1805, near the port of Cádiz and the Strait of Gibraltar. For months, the British fleet had been blockading the French and Spanish fleets in Cádiz. Admiral Pierre de Villeneuve led the French fleet. In September 1805, an order came to Villeneuve to leave Cádiz and make his way to Naples in Italy to provide backup for the French campaign. Several weeks later, Villeneuve's ships pulled out of Cádiz and began making their way to the Mediterranean Sea. His hope was to get away without engaging in any battles. But on the morning of October 21st, the

British fleet, under the command of Admiral Horatio Nelson, went after them. The British fleet approached them in two columns. Villeneuve arranged his fleet in a single line headed for the north. Britain's two columns attacked them from the west and then the center. They were able to successfully break through the enemy line. A counter-attack from some of the French and Spanish ships, which had been unaffected in the first attack, also failed. Britain's superior firepower and seamanship were too much for France and Spain and led to a decisive victory for the empire. Britain didn't lose a single ship during the battle and had less than two thousand casualties, whereas France and Spain lost a total of twenty-two ships and more than thirteen thousand men (captured, wounded, and killed). This was a hugely significant battle because the defeat dashed Napoleon's plans of an invasion of Britain and firmly cemented Britain's naval supremacy. Nelson, unfortunately, was mortally wounded.

3) **Battle of Austerlitz** – Also known as the Battle of the Three Emperors, the Battle of Austerlitz was fought on December 2nd, 1805, near a town called Austerlitz (present-day Czech Republic). The French forces were pitted against Austrian and Russian forces. Like most of the battles fought during the Napoleonic Wars, it was bloody and violent and resulted in a high number of casualties. During the battle, Napoleon caught the Austro-Russians off-guard and surprised them with an attack they were not expecting. French troops were then able to easily surround the enemy forces, and after several hours of fighting, the Austro-Russian army began to retreat. Napoleon swept in, forced Austria and Russia to sign a treaty with France, and easily took control of much of central Europe. Winning this battle solidified his dominance in Europe.

4) **Battle of Borodino** – This battle took place during France's disastrous invasion of Russia. It would become the largest and bloodiest battle of the war. At least seventy thousand casualties were suffered on both sides, which is a catastrophic number for one day of fighting. French troops launched several offensives against the Russians, who staunchly held their ground. After more than a day of fighting, the Russian army finally began to retreat, but the French were too weak to follow them. The French technically won the battle because they had captured

Moscow, which had been burned and abandoned by the Russians, but they lost their shot at winning the war against Russia. Winter soon set in, and Napoleon realized how trapped he and his men had become. The Battle of Borodino became the turning point for the Napoleonic Wars, as Russian troops eventually regrouped and launched their own counteroffensive against the French. Napoleon's army was defeated and forced to leave Russia.

5) **Battle of Waterloo** – This was the last and final battle of the Napoleonic Wars and is one of the most important battles in European history. It was fought on June 18th, 1815, near the village of Waterloo, located in present-day Belgium. It started in the morning when French troops attacked the allied forces. The fighting was intense, bloody, and lasted all day. Both sides lost a lot of lives. In the afternoon, a Prussian force that had been marching toward Waterloo to support the British finally arrived.

The Battle of Waterloo by William Sadler II.

The fresh batch of troops tipped the balance in favor of Britain and its allies, and France ultimately lost the battle. With this crushing defeat, Napoleon was forced to accept the fact that his ambitions were dead. He was forced to abdicate once again. Waterloo was hugely significant because it put an end to Napoleon's reign, ushering in a new era of relative peace and stability in Europe. It also made Britain the most powerful military force in Europe. Britain now reigned supreme on both land and sea.

Pax Britannica

The period of peace and stability that descended upon Europe during the 19th century after Napoleon's abdication and subsequent exile is referred to as Pax Britannica. The term came from an earlier term, the Pax Romana, which was used during the 1st and 2nd centuries CE to refer to the peace that existed throughout the Roman Empire.

After the Napoleonic Wars ended, Britain was the dominant European power. The empire's influence was spread around the world, while its indisputable military and economic might allowed the country to have a significant say in global affairs.

Britain's maritime control also meant it had control of key shipping and trade routes, giving the empire an automatic advantage.

In short, the British Empire was practically invincible.

Chapter 6: India: The Imperial Century

During the period of the Pax Britannica, British culture, language, values, and traditions were spread around the world. Significant advancements were made in the fields of science, technology, and medicine. The steam engine and the telegraph were some of the more notable inventions of the time.

Industrial Revolution

During the 18th and 19th centuries, Europe and North America underwent a period of significant economic and social change commonly referred to as the First Industrial Revolution.

During the early part of the 18th century, industries in Britain were small cottage industries and heavily reliant on manual labor. For example, textiles like cotton and wool were produced by people working from their homes through weaving and spinning. The process was slow, laborious, and expensive.

As new technologies started to be developed, the manufacturing process began to transition from manual labor to machines. In the textile industry, inventions like the power loom made it easier to produce clothing and required less manual labor, which quickly led to the mass production of cloths and fabrics.

Power loom.
https://commons.wikimedia.org/wiki/File:Powerloom_weaving_in_1835.jpg

Charcoal was slowly replaced with another new technique: iron ore smelted with coke. This was less expensive than charcoal and produced better-quality materials. This, in turn, helped Britain expand its iron and steel industries.

However, the one technology that changed the landscape of industries forever and had the greatest impact was steam power.

When coal mines, factories, and mills began to implement steam engines, production increased dramatically, creating new opportunities for commerce and trading. The technology also facilitated the process of mining for coal, making it easier for miners to dig deep and extract the rock.

The Industrial Revolution had a domino-like effect.

The increasing demand for coal triggered a need to revamp Britain's fairly primitive transportation system. A new network of canals near major waterways was established, and new techniques in the construction of roads were developed, increasing the number of stagecoaches traveling around the country.

By the early 1800s, steam-powered ships and locomotives began to be used, forever changing the way goods were transported in and out of the country.

Britain's social and economic landscape began to completely transform. Banks and financiers began to play a more important role in society, leading to the creation of the stock exchange in 1801.

The invention of the telegraph and the telephone made it easier than ever to communicate with people and brought the world closer together, which was important since people became more mobile during the Industrial Revolution. Britain saw a mass migration, as people left rural farming areas to settle in cities in search of job opportunities.

Cities like Liverpool and Manchester began to grow and thrive. Because of this, social changes began to take shape. There was the rise of the middle and upper middle class. Goods and items previously unattainable for the vast majority of the public were now easily accessible. Improved wages and affordability of goods meant many people enjoyed a much better quality of life than before.

However, not every aspect of the Industrial Revolution was positive. Issues like working conditions in factories and child labor also began to emerge. Living conditions for the poor continued to deteriorate. Cities saw overcrowding, a lack of sanitation, and awful housing conditions.

Labor movements were formed to fight for workers' rights and improve the lives of poorer citizens. Their fights eventually paved the way for the creation of trade unions. Child labor laws were passed, and regulations regarding public health were established. Modern-day capitalism was introduced, and the world as we know it today slowly started to take shape.

In short, we can agree that industrialization completely changed Britain's way of life and had a profound impact on the evolution of society. It transformed Britain's largely agricultural society into an industrial powerhouse. It spurred economic growth with the emergence of industries like textiles, coal mining, and iron and led to increased trading and generated more revenue for the country.

The Industrial Revolution had a significant impact on Britain's role and status in the world. The country, which was already a powerful empire by that point, now had the added might and strength of industrialization behind it, allowing it to control and exploit colonies even more than before.

Industrialization and Colonialism

Industrialization played a significant role in the second wave of colonization during the late 18th and 19th centuries. Now that factories were in a position to mass produce products, the demand for raw materials, the bulk of which arrived from the colonies, skyrocketed.

Colonies were pressured to secure these raw materials. The final products were often sold back to the colonies at a steep profit.

The slave trade continued to be an integral part of this process. It thrived and was perfected during this time. By 1860, over 12.5 million Africans had been taken captive from Africa and forced into slavery by English traders. They were then sold to plantation owners in North America and the Caribbean.

Since a large portion of the revenue generated from the slave trade was invested in Britain's industries, it became a vicious cycle where industrialization, capitalism, slavery, and colonization were all linked together.

Through industrialization, Britain eventually expanded into India as a ruler via the East India Company.

Before delving further into Britain's role in India, an important event to discuss is the Slave Trade Act of 1807, which saw the British Empire officially abolish the slave trade. Officially known as An Act for the Abolition of the Slave Trade, the act was passed after several failed attempts to abolish slavery.

By the late 1700s, many people began to question the ethics of slavery. By the 1830s, the practice was banned by countries in Europe and the Americas. However, the practice continued and even flourished, with the British transporting slaves in ships sailing under the American flag or on US ships. Around 1.65 million people were trafficked illegally in this matter during the 1800s. Historical records indicate that the last time a slave ship crossed the Atlantic Ocean was in the late 1860s. It was a ship bound for Cuba.

Enslaved people were freed almost three decades after the passage of the act in 1838, with slave owners receiving compensation for their loss. Reparations continued to be paid out until 2015. No money was paid to those who had been enslaved.

British Control in India

As discussed previously, the East India Company had been established in the 1600s to facilitate trade for Britain. It was a powerful corporation that had a monopoly on British trade, importing goods like cotton, tea, and silks from the East.

The company helped the empire extend its influence and have total control of its colonies. It was also directly responsible for Britain's rule in India.

For centuries, India had been ruled by the Mughal Empire, but by the 1700s, the empire was beginning to crumble. Things came to a head during the reign of Muhammad Shah between 1719 and 1748. Infighting, rebellions, and battles with the Marathas, a warrior group from present-day Maharashtra in India, all led to the fragmentation of the Mughal Empire.

The period of instability and weakness made it difficult for the empire to resist the growing power of the East India Company. The company firmly established its presence and control by establishing key alliances with Indian rulers and the military and by employing a strategy of divide and conquer. The British exploited the rivalries and conflicts between the different groups, kingdoms, and sects in India, ensuring they remained divided.

The turning point of British colonization in India took place after the Battle of Plassey. It was fought between the nawab of Bengal, Siraj-ud-Daulah, and the East India Company when the company tried to further expand into Bengal. The British had been doing this for some time, and the nawab refused to allow them to go any further. He was angry that the company refused to pay them any taxes and at how it openly flouted his authority.

The battle took place on June 23rd, 1757. The pro-French Siraj-ud-Daulah was supported by France. The nawab had an army of fifty thousand men with additional artillerymen sent by the French.

British forces, led by Robert Clive, fought viciously, opening fire on the army and killing hundreds. When the nawab began to retreat, the British were easily able to capture the French artillery. They eventually won the battle.

Robert Clive by Nathanial Dance-Holland.

The company's victory marked the beginning of Britain's rule over India, which would last for almost two hundred years. In the decades that followed, the East India Company rapidly expanded its territories and influence by using military force, forging political alliances, and using economic exploitation. By the middle of the 19th century, the East India Company had absolute control over most of India.

Regulating Act of 1773

As the East India Company began to gain more political power and control in India, concerns began to emerge over corruption and mismanagement within the company. To regulate its activities and holdings, the British Parliament passed the Regulating Act in 1773.

Several provisions were established as a result of the act. A few key ones include:

- Creation of a governor-general of Bengal position. This role was given general authority over the activities of the East India Company, as well as control over the company's military forces.
- Creation of the Supreme Council to oversee the company's

activities. The council was made up of the governor-general and four other members.
- Curtailing the company's ability to trade at will. The purpose of restricting trade activities was to limit the company's power and reach.
- Accepting gifts or bribery from anyone or engaging in personal trade was also prohibited under the act.

Each provision was designed to prevent the company from increasing its power and influence. It was a significant milestone since it was the British government's first attempt to rein in the company and control its activities.

However, despite the government's best intentions, the act was flawed. The power and authority of the Supreme Council were not defined clearly, and the reports sent by the governor-general did not go anywhere.

Corruption within the company and high-level officials continued.

India Act of 1784

In an attempt to fix the flaws in the Regulating Act of 1773, new legislation was passed by Parliament in 1784.

Named after Britain's prime minister, William Pitt, Pitt's India Act established a system of "dual control" in India to separate commercial activities and political issues. It gave the British government control over the East India Company's activities and administration in India. The government was given veto power, as well as rights to the company's financial transactions. The act also sought to expand trade by placing fewer restrictions on Indian goods imported to Britain.

Two boards were created to ensure the provisions of the new act were enforced: the Board of Control, which represented the British government, and the Court of Directors, which represented the company.

The Board of Control was tasked with overseeing and monitoring the company's policies, while the Court of Directors was to oversee the company's commercial operations.

Pitt's act was a huge improvement from the previous one, and it was far more successful. However, problems continued to linger.

Charter Act of 1813

A third attempt at addressing the problems with the East India Company was made in 1813 with the passing of the Charter Act. This act would have a significant impact on trade and education.

Under this act, the East India Company's authority in India was extended for another two decades; however, its trade monopoly was eliminated, with the only exception being goods traded with China, such as tea and opium. All other trade in India was opened up to all British subjects.

It also cemented the British monarchy's sovereignty over India and strengthened the power of Indian courts and provincial governments.

When the Charter Act was passed, an annual allocation of 100,000 rupees (the equivalent of $1,200 USD) was granted to improve education and literacy in India. For the first time, legislation was implemented that gave Indians the right to an education.

In the past, both the East India Company and the British Parliament had been against the idea of exposing foreign religions to Indians. Missionaries were forbidden from coming into the country to push forward religious ideas. It was feared the native population might feel threatened by conversions, which would have been detrimental to Britain's trade pursuits.

When the act passed, large groups of missionaries arrived in India and established schools and educational institutions. Many of these English schools provided the foundation of India's modern educational system.

Indian Rebellion of 1857

The Indian Rebellion is often called India's First War of Independence or the Sepoy Mutiny. The revolt against the British, which started on May 10th, 1857, and ended over two years later on July 8th, 1859, had widespread support but was unsuccessful.

Tensions between India and Britain had been simmering for some time. As Britain became increasingly entrenched in every aspect of India, the native population grew restless and resentful. They were angry at being subjected to British rule, they were upset over taxation, and they were tired of having their workers, farmers, and craftsmen exploited for the benefit of the British.

Cultural and religious differences were also becoming a cause of frustration, as Indians feared their beliefs and practices were under threat. Hindu princely states and the Indian aristocratic class were being replaced by white British people. Plum positions were given to the British, land was annexed and taken away, and there was a general sense the British were taking over.

The resentment came to a head when a new rifle cartridge was introduced by the British to be used by the sepoys (Indian soldiers who were recruited locally to form a part of the British army). They were armed and trained like European soldiers and fought in battalions. However, they were not treated with the same respect and dignity as the white soldiers. Sepoys were underpaid and overworked. They were subjected to daily abuse and racism from the British.

When the new cartridges were made, there were rumors that they were greased with fat from cows and pigs, which offended the majority of the native population. For Hindus, the cow is a sacred animal, and Islam considers pigs to be an unclean animal.

When the new rifles came out, they were told to load them by biting on the ends of the cartridge with their teeth, which they could not do since putting pig and cow fat on their mouths went against their religious beliefs. They found this unacceptable and disrespectful. Thus, the cartridges became the tipping point that sparked a rebellion, even though no evidence has emerged that the British used animal fat to grease them.

In April 1857, sepoys stationed at Meerut refused to use the new cartridges. They were taken away in shackles and given long prison sentences. On May 10th, other sepoys, angry at this injustice, banded together. They rebelled against the British officers by shooting them and made their way to Delhi.

Sepoy revolt at Meerut from Illustrated London News, 1857.
https://commons.wikimedia.org/wiki/File:The_Sepoy_revolt_at_Meerut.jpg

Delhi had no European troops, so it was easier to join forces with the Meerut men and seize the city. Within the day, Mughal Emperor Bahadur Shah II was restored to power. The rebellion quickly spread to other parts of northern India. Unfortunately for the mutineers, most of the princes and other Indian leaders steered clear of the mutiny.

The British moved quickly and effectively to snuff out the mutiny. It was a vicious and bloody rebellion. The mutineers massacred the British, and the British bayoneted sepoys or had them shot from cannons.

It is estimated that around six thousand British were killed during the mutiny. The number on the Indian side is far higher at an estimated 800,000 deaths.

Even though India lost the rebellion, it led to a significant reshuffling of how things were managed in India. The East India Company's rule was abolished, and control of the country was transferred directly to the British government. A conscious decision was made to include Indians in consultations and communicate with them more on key decisions. A new council with more Indian representation was established in 1861 to replace the previous one made up entirely of white Europeans.

The British also backtracked on many of the social measures they had imposed that Indians had found upsetting. But even though the British tried to be more "open," they became more controlling and oppressive because they wanted to prevent another rebellion.

Within Indian society, the realization that they would never be able to recapture a past without British influence began to set in. India's social structure began to see a shift as a Westernized class emerged.

However, the failed rebellion was also a major turning point for Indian nationalism, and the desire to be free started to become even stronger.

Government of India Act of 1858

In response to the Sepoy Mutiny, the Government of India Act was passed in 1858. This act put an end to the East India Company's power and rule in India, giving direct control of the country to the British Crown. A new office was established under the act: the secretary of state for India. This office reported directly to the British Parliament and was tasked with the administration of India.

A council of advisors was tasked with the responsibility of advising the secretary on what was happening in India.

India's political structure was also reshaped with the act. The country was divided into provinces, each one headed by a governor. The provinces themselves were then divided into districts, with a district officer at the head.

New laws and regulations aligned with British values and standards were introduced in India. The goal was to modernize the country and make it more "Western."

No doubt, the act and the ousting of the East India Company did improve some things in India. However, the exploitation of resources and oppression of the population continued to increase as Britain worked hard to maintain absolute control of the country and its people.

To further their agenda, the British government pitted Hindus and Muslims against each other and tried to physically separate the two in 1905 by dividing Bengal into Muslim and Hindu sections. They revoked this after protests from both sides.

British Raj

After the rebellion ended and Britain became India's direct ruler, a new period referred to as the British Raj emerged. This period lasted from 1858 to 1947, and during this time, India was subject to British rule, government, and administration.

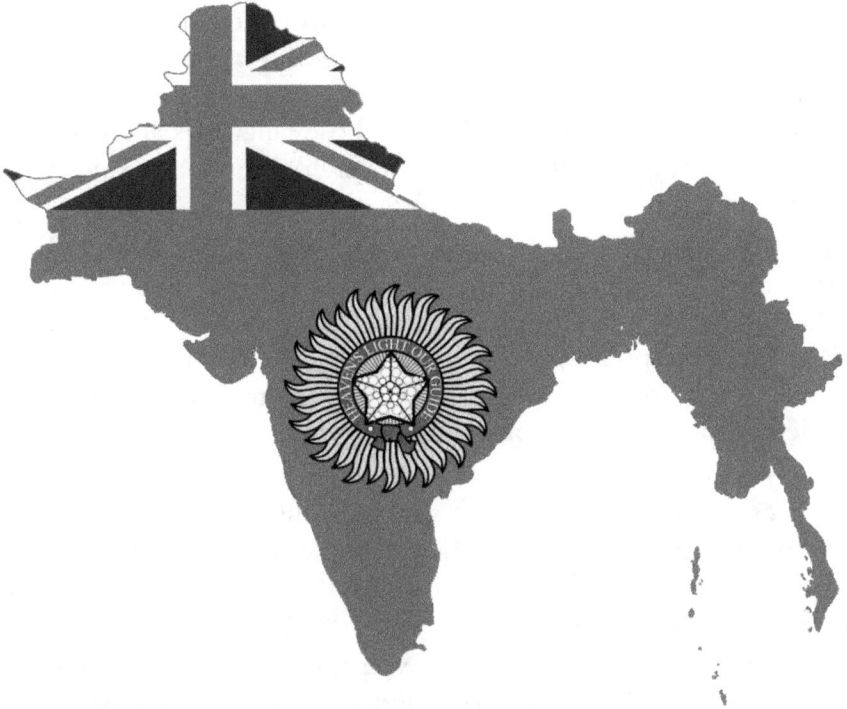

The goal of the British Raj was to ensure that Indians were able to participate in the governing of their own country, but the reality was Indians were mostly powerless to determine anything about their future. The highest positions of power were held by British officials. For example, the viceroy of India, who was the head of the colonial government, was appointed by the British monarch.

Under the British Raj, a system of indirect rule was established in which Indian princes and local rulers were allowed to govern their own territories as long as they pledged loyalty to the British Crown. But this was often a "surface" rule, as the Indian leaders often had very little power and had to follow whatever British officials wanted.

During this time, India underwent significant changes, both positive and negative. Because of British rule, India saw modern technology, a better education system, and improved infrastructure, all of which helped to modernize the country.

English was introduced as the language of education and governance, which helped to unify the country and establish a common language for communication. This was key since India had 179 different languages and 544 dialects at one point. Many of those languages and dialects have been wiped away. Today, India has over four hundred languages and dialects.

There were plenty of negatives as well. The British Raj was characterized by exploitation and oppression. Heavy taxes were imposed on the Indian population without a care for their economic well-being. This led to widespread poverty, famine, and hardship. The British also created a lot of issues between the different ethnic and religious groups in order to maintain their control of the region.

The period saw the emergence of a new class: people who grew up with Western values and ideas, spoke fluent English, and received a Western education. Many of these people were determined to gain independence for their country and would go on to play an important role in Indian politics and shape modern-day India.

Following years of struggle by nationalists and independence movements, India finally gained its independence on August 15th, 1947, officially bringing an end to the British Raj.

Scramble for Africa

During the late 19th century, even as the British Empire began to show cracks, the Scramble for Africa began in earnest.

European powers like France, Germany, Italy, Portugal, Spain, and Great Britain became embroiled once more in a furious race to claim and colonize as much of Africa as they could.

This scramble is also referred to as the African Partition or the Conquest of Africa.

The goal of the European powers was to expand their influence across the African continent and gain more territories. More often than not, these conquests were achieved through military force.

The division of the continent was formalized through the Berlin Conference of 1884–1885, also known as the Congo Conference. During this conference, European colonial powers met together in Berlin with one goal: to resolve the territorial claims in Africa.

Berlin Conference – 1884.
https://commons.wikimedia.org/wiki/File:Kongokonferenz.jpg

The European powers had to prove they had control over the territories they had claimed in order to legitimize ownership. By the end of the meeting, Africa had been divided between fourteen European nations.

They agreed on the rules for division, as well as regulations on trade and colonization. The sovereignty of the Congo Free State, which had been under the rule of King Leopold II of Belgium, was also recognized during the conference.

The African partition and Europe's scramble for a slice of the continent would have lasting repercussions for the African people. Their way of life, culture, and ethnic values were all destroyed by the colonial powers. Their resources were depleted, and their wealth was stolen.

The plundering and exploitation by the European powers created a divide and plunged the African countries into centuries of conflict, poverty, and instability.

Today, nineteen African countries are still part of the British Commonwealth: Botswana, Cameroon, Ghana, Kenya, Lesotho, Malawi, Mauritius, Mozambique, Namibia, Nigeria, Rwanda, Seychelles, Sierra Leone, South Africa, Swaziland, Uganda, United Republic of

Tanzania, and Zambia. With the passing of Queen Elizabeth II and the crowing of Charles III as king, there is a growing movement and desire in these countries to pull away from the monarchy and become republics.

Chapter 7: The Empire during the World Wars

First World War

On July 28th, 1914, when World War I broke out, Britain was a power to be reckoned with, both in Europe and around the world. A quarter of the world was under the country's rule. Britain had a powerful, dominant navy, an impressive military force, and a strong and stable economy. In every way, Britain was viewed as the largest and mightiest global power.

Initially, Britain's role in WWI was limited. The British were only there to provide support to France and Russia while they fought Germany. Because the United States was still practicing its policy of isolationism, they were not involved, so Britain had to step in to play the protector role. As the war escalated, the nation's role morphed from supporter to leader, with Britain playing a crucial role in the Allied victory against the Central Powers.

One of Britain's most significant contributions to the war effort was its impressive navy. It was instrumental in blockading Germany and preventing the nation from moving critical supplies and troops. This significantly weakened Germany's position and hampered its war efforts.

HMS Satyr, which served during WWI.
https://en.wikipedia.org/wiki/File:HMS_Satyr_1916.jpg

British troops also played a vital role on the Western Front. Their tanks, weapons, artillery, military strategies, and commanders contributed to the Allied success in the trenches against the Germans.

The war effort was further aided by Britain's strong economy. During the war, the nation's industrial output increased rapidly, with factories churning out munitions, weapons, and other crucial wartime supplies. As men went to fight in the war, women stepped into traditionally male roles, allowing the economy to thrive.

Sykes-Picot Agreement

Historically, Britain and France had never been friends. Throughout the centuries, they had a tumultuous relationship, sometimes battling wars and stealing territories and other times maintaining a cool indifference toward each other.

However, by the time WWI broke out, Britain became one of France's most important allies. The two realized they needed to be united if they wanted to defeat the Central Powers, which primarily consisted of Germany, Austria-Hungary, and the Ottoman Empire.

France and Britain became such strong allies that they even drafted a secret agreement to divide up the Middle East between themselves once the war was over. The Sykes-Picot Agreement was named after the two diplomats who negotiated the terms of the treaty.

Prior to the treaty being drafted, during the summer of 1914, numerous discussions about the Ottoman Empire were held, mainly about what would happen to the territory once Germany and its allies were defeated. After much discussion, in 1915, a secret agreement was signed with Russia, where Russia would be given Constantinople, the capital city of the Ottoman Empire.

A year after that, on May 19th, 1916, the Sykes-Picot Agreement was drafted. Under the agreement, both Britain and France would be given parts of the Middle East, placing them under their spheres of influence. Most of present-day Syria and Lebanon were given to France, while Britain was given Iraq, Jordan, and Kuwait. A designated zone of international control was established, which included Palestine.

It would be up to each country to decide how they wished to rule or administer their regions. The countries also agreed that trade and passage would flow freely between their spheres.

Arab nationalism was not given any consideration in these discussions. In fact, this agreement went against the promises made by Britain to the Arabs to give them self-determination and independence in exchange for their support against the Ottomans.

In 1917, the agreement was leaked, and both France and Britain faced a lot of criticism from the Arab world. Nevertheless, the agreement went ahead anyway, and it led to the drawing of new borders of the defeated Ottoman Empire's territory, creating the modern-day Middle East.

The Arabs, who felt betrayed by the agreement, began to demand independence. Instability and conflicts have plagued the Arab nations since. Many of the ongoing issues and battles embroiling the Middle East today, especially between Israel and Palestine, can be traced back to the Sykes-Picot Agreement.

Britain and the Allied Powers

In addition to the alliance with France, Britain also developed key alliances with Russia and Italy. Geographically, Russia was located at the opposite end of the continent, but it was perfectly positioned to provide a buffer against Germany on the Eastern Front.

Italy had initially been in a pact with Germany and Austria-Hungary, known as the Triple Alliance, but when the war started, Italy decided to play the waiting game and remained neutral.

A year later, in 1915, Britain successfully managed to convince Italy to support the Allied effort by offering territories in the Adriatic Sea, including Tyrol, Trieste, and Istria. With this agreement in place, Italy entered the war on the Allied side.

After years of providing financial and military support to the Allies, the United States formally declared war on the Central Powers in 1917.

Creating an alliance with these countries and pooling resources and military strategies together was key to the Allied victory in WWI.

The British Empire and the War

WWI wasn't just a European conflict; it was a global war that touched nearly every corner of the world.

Most of the European powers fighting in the war had far-flung colonies and territories under their rule, and they called on these colonies to aid the war effort.

The British Empire was massive at this time, and it was able to recruit soldiers from North America, Australia, Europe, Africa, and Asia (that's five of the seven continents!). In total, approximately two and a half million men were sent from the colonies to fight with the British. Countries like Bangladesh, South Africa, Zimbabwe, Canada, and Australia all sent soldiers.

Battle of the Somme, which included troops from Canada.
https://commons.wikimedia.org/wiki/File:Wiltshire_Regiment_Thiepval_7_August_1916.jpg

Aside from the enormous amount of human power that Britain was able to gather, the war effort was also aided by an abundance of resources extracted from the colonies. For instance, Canada was a major producer of food and timber for the Allies, while India provided the troops with raw materials like cotton and tea. New Zealand and Australia kept them supplied with meat and wool. These colonies also provided naval support to the British, sending contingents to serve in the Mediterranean and the North Sea.

The colonies were also used to circulate propaganda, which highlighted the Allied cause and made it clear who the real villain was. Posters, films, and other media encouraged people to support the war, provided a justification for why resources and materials were needed, and helped to recruit soldiers.

There is no doubt the war would have been harder to win (if at all) without the support, aid, and strength of the colonies. Britain's skill in rallying the colonies to the Allied cause has to be noted because it was no small feat. The same feat was achieved during the Second World War, which will be discussed later.

Interwar Period

After World War I ended, a period referred to as the interbellum or interwar period followed.

Significant political, economic, and social changes swept through the world. Nothing was quite the way it had been prior to July 1914, and each of these changes slowly chipped away at the power and might of the British Empire.

The war had also left the world in shambles, triggering a widespread desire for peace and stability, even as political ideologies and movements like fascism, communism, and Nazism arose.

Social unrest was further exacerbated by the Great Depression in the 1930s, which provided the perfect setting for authoritarian regimes to emerge in several countries around the world.

The peacekeeping efforts of the Allied countries soon started to crumble amid rising tensions and petty conflicts, eventually triggering the Second World War.

Treaty of Versailles

The Treaty of Versailles, signed on June 28th, 1919, brought a formal end to WWI. The peace terms were drafted and negotiated by the victorious Allies, with Britain playing a key role in shaping the final treaty.

The three men primarily credited with the treaty were British Prime Minister David Lloyd George, French Prime Minister Georges Clemenceau, and President Woodrow Wilson from the United States. Vittorio Emanuele Orlando of Italy was also present. Together, these men are known as the "Big Four."

The Big Four at the Paris Peace Conference, May 1919.
https://commons.wikimedia.org/wiki/File:Big_four.jpg

Britain's main objectives during the treaty negotiations were to protect its colonies and imperial interests, maintain the balance of power in Europe, and punish Germany in such a way that it would never again dare to repeat its past actions.

The terms of the treaty included the following:

- Germany had to dramatically reduce its military to 100,000 men. All the men had to be volunteers since conscription was banned. Tanks, submarines, and aircraft were also banned. The Germans were only allowed to keep six battleships, six light cruisers, and twelve destroyers. Basically, the Allies wanted to remove Germany as a military threat.
- Germany was forced to accept full responsibility for the war and had to pay enormous sums of money in reparations to the Allies, mainly France and Belgium. Both provisions were a

huge blow to the country's pride.

- Germany had to cede territories to the Allies.
- The treaty included a provision to establish the League of Nations. This was an international organization tasked with promoting cooperation among nations and snuffing out conflicts peacefully before they could escalate.

As expected, Germany did not take kindly to the terms of the treaty, but it was powerless to argue against it. Germany's anger and resentment of the treaty would simmer over the decades that followed, and ironically, the treaty would become one of the contributors to WWII.

A Commonwealth of Nations

During the interwar period, many British colonies began to seek more autonomy and desired sovereignty. Unable or unwilling to cut ties with Britain completely, several former colonies got together to establish an association in 1931. They called themselves the Commonwealth of Nations.

They were independent states that recognized the British monarchy as their symbolic head and chose to develop ties of friendship and cooperation with one another. Participation was purely voluntary.

One of the key traits of the British Commonwealth was that each member was treated as an equal. The size or level of development of the nation did not matter; everyone was on an equal footing. This was a significant shift from the imperial relationship each member state had had with Britain.

Members were also not tied to one another in any legal or formal way through a constitution or bylaws, unlike other international bodies.

Countries like Canada, Australia, South Africa, and Britain were the early members of the Commonwealth. Over the next few years and decades, more countries, including India, Ghana, Sierra Leone, Singapore, and Barbados, joined the Commonwealth.

The association became an important forum for diplomatic and economic cooperation among the member states. While British influence was still strong, for the first time, these countries had a platform to express their own concerns and consider their own interests.

Through the British Commonwealth, other institutions like the Commonwealth Secretariat and the Commonwealth Games were developed, which were designed to foster cooperation and ties of friendship between member states.

Since the Commonwealth's inception, the member states have faced many challenges. There have been tensions, disagreements, and fundamental differences of opinion. However, they managed to push through those issues and continue to play an important role in international politics today.

Over the last nine decades, many countries seeking complete independence have left the Commonwealth. Others, like Barbados, became a republic within the Commonwealth. Today, fifty-six countries make up the Commonwealth.

Partition of the Ottoman Empire

For centuries, the Ottoman Empire had been a powerful force in the Middle East and southwestern Europe, but by the early 20th century, the empire was in decline.

During the First World War, the Ottoman Empire made the decision to side with Germany and the Central Powers. When they were defeated, the Allies looked at how the territory within the Ottoman Empire could be divided among themselves. This would kickstart the West's dominance and influence in the region.

The partition and redrawing of the Ottoman Empire's political boundaries were formalized through a series of treaties, including the Treaty of Sèvres and the Treaty of Lausanne.

Britain played a key role in the negotiations that led to the division of the empire. Under the Treaty of Sèvres, which was signed on August 10th, 1920, the Ottoman Empire was disarmed, subjected to harsh reparations, and had to give up territories.

Political boundaries were redrawn, and new states were created, including Syria, Lebanon, Iraq, and Jordan.

Treaty of Sèvres

Map according to the Treaty of Sèvres.

Zero0000, CC BY-SA 4.0 <https://creativecommons.org/licenses/by-sa/4.0>, via Wikimedia Commons; https://commons.wikimedia.org/wiki/File:SevresTreaty.png

Nationalist forces in Turkey, led by military officer Mustafa Kemal Pasha (later known as Atatürk), refused to accept the treaty and launched a resistance movement against the Allied Powers. This resistance snowballed into the Turkish War of Independence and the establishment of modern-day Turkey, with Atatürk as president.

Since the Treaty of Sèvres had never been ratified and had failed in its objective, a new treaty was drafted: the Treaty of Lausanne. This peace agreement was signed on July 24th, 1923, by Turkey, which became the Ottoman Empire's successor, and the Allied Powers, bringing an end to the Turkish War of Independence and recognizing the country as a sovereign, democratic nation. It also included provisions to protect the rights of Greek Christian minorities who lived in Turkey and Muslim minority groups who lived in Greece.

In exchange, Turkey recognized that Cyprus was a British possession and renounced its claims to the Dodecanese Islands, which Italy had occupied during the Italo-Turkish War of 1912. In 1919 and 1920, discussions between Italy and Greece about ceding these islands occurred. However, due to the ongoing war between Greece and Turkey, which lasted from 1912 to 1922, the agreement was never formalized. In 1923, the islands were formally annexed by Italy instead of going to Greece.

Borders of Turkey based on the Treaty of Lausanne.

While the partition gave Britain significant control over the Middle East, providing the country with new strategic and economic opportunities, it also came with a lot of headaches, as Britain struggled to maintain stability in the region while pursuing its own imperial interests.

The redrawn boundaries caused a lot of problems, as they did not take into account key factors like ethnicity, religion, or the culture of the people living within the boundaries. People were opposed to being under British rule, and the strong desire for independence led to the rise of Arab nationalist movements.

Palestine proved to be an especially problematic region for Britain. In 1917, under the terms of the Balfour Declaration, Britain promised the Jewish people a homeland in Palestinian territory in exchange for support during WWI.

It's unclear how Britain expected to manage two nations sharing a territory that was sacred to both Muslims and Jews, but the tensions and conflicts between the two nations started soon after. In 1948, British rule in Palestine officially ended, and tensions with Israel, which had been created on May 14th, 1948, escalated rapidly.

Over the decades, Palestine has been shrinking, with Israel occupying more and more of the land. Western nations, mainly the United States, have tried to find an amicable solution without success. The conflict is largely overlooked by Western nations, with most supporting and recognizing Israel as an independent nation. There are also countries that refuse to accept Israel's existence, mostly in the Arab world, because of how it was created and the impact it has had on Palestine and other Arab countries.

It's impossible to know whether British and Allied interference in the Middle East made things worse or better for the Arabs. What we do know definitively is that taking control of the Middle East, which is rich in natural resources, namely oil, has been enormously beneficial to many Western nations. We also know the region is plagued with endless conflicts, instability, and wars, most of which are rooted in the treaties and agreements drafted by Western nations.

Second World War

Britain's Role

Britain's position, both internationally and at home, was profoundly impacted by the war. The threat of Hitler had started several years before World War II officially started. It was becoming increasingly clear to the world that Hitler was taking strategic steps toward an unknown end goal. But desperate to avoid another war, most countries turned a blind eye to his movements.

Adolf Hitler, 1933.
Bundesarchiv, Bild 146-1990-048-29A / CC-BY-SA 3.0, CC BY-SA 3.0 DE
<*https://creativecommons.org/licenses/by-sa/3.0/de/deed.en*>, *via Wikimedia Commons;*
https://commons.wikimedia.org/wiki/File:Adolf_Hitler_Berghof-1936.jpg

However, when Germany invaded Poland on September 1ˢᵗ, 1939, both Britain and France declared war on Germany two days later.

Hitler moved quickly, defeating and invading country after country. By the summer of 1940, he had successfully invaded Poland, Norway, Denmark, Belgium, and the Netherlands.

In May 1940, he turned his attention to France.

Once France was defeated and invaded by the Nazis, Britain, supported by its colonies, was left to fend off Germany mostly on its own, as key allies like Russia and the United States joined the war later.

Nevertheless, Britain did a formidable job of trying to curtail Hitler's advances. Prime Minister Winston Churchill, in particular, was a key player during the war, leading the country through an extremely dark period.

Long before the war broke out, Winston Churchill had his eye on Hitler, and he warned the world that the Nazis could become extremely dangerous for Europe. Recognizing that a war might happen, he started to covertly prepare Britain for it.

When the war did break out, he demonstrated incredible leadership. He inspired and mobilized the British people, built alliances with other powers, and was heavily involved in strategic military campaigns, such as the D-Day landings and the North Africa campaign.

Churchill was also a strong advocate of using bombs against Germany and encouraged the British Royal Air Force to increase bombing raids on German cities.

Under his guidance and leadership, Churchill united the various political groups and politicians to defeat their common enemy, Nazi Germany.

Winston Churchill and his contributions to the war are discussed in more detail in Chapter 9.

Battle of Britain

By the time Hitler looked to invade Britain, he had already conquered much of Europe. Britain was the last piece standing between him and the domination of the entire continent. As a prelude to the invasion, he wanted to decimate the Royal Air Force (RAF).

On July 10ᵗʰ, 1940, the German Luftwaffe launched a series of attacks against Britain. The RAF responded in kind with its own fighter planes.

Britain's advanced radar technology and intelligence were key advantages, which they used to successfully ward off the Luftwaffe.

Germany conducted a series of targeted bombings referred to as the Blitz. The bomb raids razed cities to the ground and killed tens of thousands of people, but the British did not give up.

German Luftwaffe flying over East London.
https://commons.wikimedia.org/wiki/File:Heinkel_He_111_over_Wapping,_East_London.jpg

By the fall of 1940, Hitler was forced to face reality. The Luftwaffe had failed to gain control of Britain's air space. But rather than admit defeat, he decided to postpone the invasion of Britain and move east toward Russia.

The Battle of Britain, as it became known, was considered to be a crucial turning point in the war and demonstrated Britain's resilience, determination, and military strength. Britain had faced the enemy alone and had defeated them. Even though Britain did not have any nations formally supporting her during the battle, a significant number of RAF pilots volunteered to serve and had been recruited from British colonies like Australia and Canada.

Impact of WWII on Britain

When the war first started, Britain took on the role of leader and protector. It fearlessly stood up to the Nazis. Britain's armed forces were the envy of the world, but by the time the war ended, it was a different story.

The British Empire had already been struggling for some time. World War II became the decisive moment in history when the empire started to decline in earnest. Britain's days of imperial dominance were well and truly left behind.

During the war, the Allied nations had only one goal in mind: defeat the Nazis. Nothing else mattered. The countries put practically everything they had into achieving this goal.

When the war finally ended on September 2nd, 1945, and the dust had settled, the actual toll of the war was revealed.

Dresden after a bombing during WWII.
Bundesarchiv, Bild 146-1994-041-07 / Unknown author / CC-BY-SA 3.0, CC BY-SA 3.0 DE
<https://creativecommons.org/licenses/by-sa/3.0/de/deed.en>, via Wikimedia Commons;
https://commons.wikimedia.org/wiki/File:Bundesarchiv_Bild_146-1994-041-
07,_Dresden,_zerst%C3%B6rtes_Stadtzentrum.jpg

For Britain, the Allied victory was overshadowed by the challenges it faced at home. Fighting the war had left Britain's economy crippled, and the country was in heavy debt. A shortage of skilled laborers made the task of rebuilding Britain's war-torn infrastructure much harder.

Hundreds and thousands of soldiers and civilians lost their lives. Cities had been destroyed by bombs, and the country was facing shortages in everything from food to everyday essentials.

To address some of these challenges, a series of policies were pushed forward by the government to stimulate economic growth. These included the nationalization of key industries and taking part in the Marshall Plan. The Marshall Plan was an economic aid program designed by the United States. Under this plan, the US provided grants, loans, and other assistance to participating countries so they could rebuild their economies and countries.

As the threat of Nazism faded, the US recognized that communism would be the next big threat, and they wanted Western European nations to be economically stable to prevent the spread of communism.

Britain also faced a lot of social changes during and after the war. Women had played an important role in both world wars, and they no longer wanted to stay at home in their "traditional" roles. They had proved themselves to be more than capable in the workforce. There was a greater push for gender equality and other social reforms.

British women working in factories during WWII.
https://commons.wikimedia.org/wiki/File:Locomotive_fast_freight_cleaning.png

The Labor Party was established in 1900, and the concept of the welfare state, which aimed to provide for those in need, came about soon after.

Art, literature, and cultural attitudes also evolved in postwar Britain. The social and political changes that took place after the war would shape future generations.

Decolonization

However, the biggest impact on Britain after the war ended was on its empire.

The years leading up to WWII had seen a rise in ideologies and political movements, and once the war was over, these movements only became stronger. Many of Britain's colonies and territories clamored for independence. Britain's hold on its colonies weakened dramatically, as did its global position.

As more colonies began to gain independence, Britain's international prestige plummeted further, as it lost access to key resources and markets at a time when it badly needed money.

When India, Britain's most prestigious colony, started to push for independence, it marked the end of an era for British imperialism. Often referred to as Britain's "crown jewel," the populous and wealthy Indian colony had played a key role in Britain's economic prosperity. But after decades under British rule, Indians wanted to be independent and free. It was a devastating blow to the British Empire.

For centuries, Britain had been the most powerful empire in the world. The British had imposed their values, their culture, and their way of living on many parts of the globe. And then, suddenly, its power rapidly eroded, its world superpower status was gone, and its ability to rebuild its own nation was heavily dependent on foreign aid and assistance.

Seeing strong, powerful countries like the United States and Russia taking over as global leaders and vying for superpower status must have been difficult for Britain to accept because it meant its time in the sun had reached an end.

Chapter 8: The Setting Sun

The comparison of the British Empire to a setting sun is believed to have been coined by various authors as early as the 1800s. After WWII, it became a metaphor for Britain's rise and eventual demise as a global superpower in the aftermath of the Second World War.

In the new postwar world, Britain found itself facing an unfamiliar environment, one it did not know how to navigate. The tactics and strategies it had used for centuries to dominate the world held no weight against the United States and Russia, the world's new rising superpowers.

Britain was virtually bankrupt and riddled with debt. Its infrastructure was in shambles, it was facing shortages at every turn, and it had to contend with social unrest both at home and abroad, with colonies demanding independence.

Britain fought hard to maintain its international standing and remain on equal footing with the US, but since it was faced with challenges from every end, it became increasingly difficult to do so. In the ensuing decades, a series of international conflicts and setbacks further exacerbated the empire's decline.

Partition of India – 1947

The British and, by extension, the East India Company and the British Raj had been ruling India since the mid-19th century. As we saw in previous chapters, the native population wasn't entirely happy with this. Tensions slowly simmered until they boiled over into outright rebellion and uprisings. The Indians had a fierce desire to overthrow what they viewed as a controlling power.

The failed rebellion in 1857 had only strengthened the idea of Indian nationalism, and by the early 1900s, the demand for independence only grew louder, with men like Mahatma Gandhi leading the movement.

Gandhi was a political and spiritual leader who employed and encouraged nonviolent civil disobedience to protest Britain's colonial rule. He believed in peaceful resistance and campaigns, emphasizing the power of moral persuasion.

Gandhi during a peaceful march in 1930.
https://commons.wikimedia.org/wiki/File:Marche_sel.jpg

His beliefs and methods of resistance landed him in jail numerous times, but he didn't give up. Over time, his philosophy and leadership mobilized millions of Indians throughout the country and shifted people's opinions in India and around the world.

By the time WWII ended, India's independence movement had gained considerable momentum, and the British government knew it would have no other choice than to grant India independence.

Before doing so, the British government, led by Prime Minister Clement Attlee, decided to partition India into two separate states based on religion. There would be a Hindu state and a Muslim state.

Officially, the government explained the partition as a way of mitigating any potential violence or unrest within India after its independence. The government was concerned that given the deep religious divisions between Hindus and Muslims, conflict and chaos might ensue once the British left.

However, historians believe the real reason for the partition was to create a weaker state. A divided India would be easier to control, and the creation of a new state, Pakistan, would allow the British to maintain their presence in the region. The British likely hoped that Pakistan would remain more closely aligned with British values and interests.

The partition of India was announced on June 3rd, 1947, and the two states were formalized on August 15th, 1947. Similar to the division of the Ottoman Empire, very little thought was given to culture, language, or social ties. The partition was simply drawn along religious lines, with Muslim areas going to Pakistan and the majority of Hindus remaining in India.

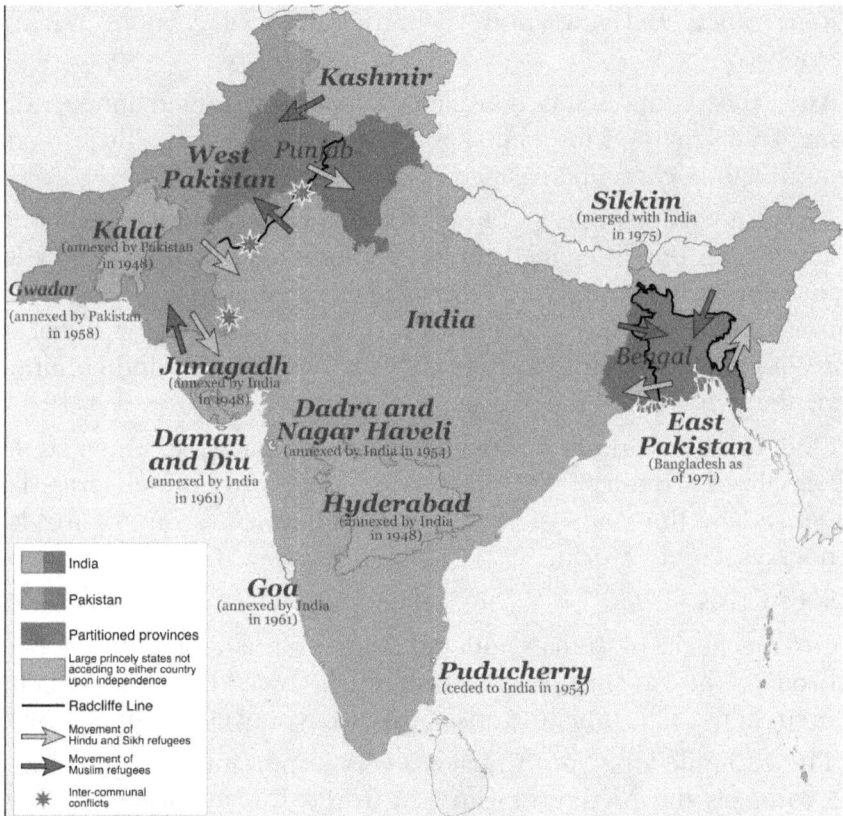

Partition of India.

Own work, CC BY-SA 4.0 <https://creativecommons.org/licenses/by-sa/4.0>, via Wikimedia Commons; https://commons.wikimedia.org/wiki/File:Partition_of_India_1947_en.svg

The partition of India became a heavily criticized decision and was met with widespread protests and violence. Millions of people were forcibly displaced. They lost their homes, their livelihood, their communities, and their way of life. Hundreds of thousands of others lost their lives.

To make things worse, the borders between the two countries were not clearly defined by the British, leading to territorial disputes. A key region that continues to be under dispute today is Kashmir. During the partition, Kashmir was given the choice of going to India or Pakistan. The ruler of Kashmir, Maharaja Hari Singh, tried to stay neutral, but he eventually decided on India.

Pakistan was against this decision and sent troops into Kashmir. This would be the start of the Indo-Pakistan War. Kashmir was eventually divided between the two states, but conflicts over the area have been ongoing since 1947, as both countries want the entire region for themselves.

After the partition was complete, India was granted independence. Losing India marked the end of Britain's colonial rule, and the empire continued to become increasingly fragmented.

Again, it's impossible to know whether the partition of India was a good decision or if it created more problems. What we do know is that the division of the country and the displacement of so many people were traumatic. It irrevocably changed the course of history for India, is the cause of ongoing tensions between Pakistan and India, and continues to shape the dynamics of the region.

Once India worked through its growing pains, it emerged as an industrialized country with a thriving economy, which was largely influenced by the years of British rule. Today, it is one of the largest democracies in the world.

Suez Crisis – 1956

On the heels of India's independence, Britain once again became embroiled in a historical event that would have long-lasting repercussions. This time, the crisis was in Egypt over the Suez Canal.

The 120-mile-long Suez Canal is a very important manmade waterway that connects the Mediterranean Sea to the Indian Ocean. It provides the quickest way of shipping goods from Europe to Asia and vice versa.

Construction of the canal began in 1859 under the joint authority of the French and British governments. Directing and supervising the build was Ferdinand de Lesseps, a French diplomat.

A decade later, in 1869, the canal was finally completed and ready to be used. While France and Britain controlled the canal and profited from its gains, Egypt was only given a small percentage of the revenue, which started to become a source of tension.

Port Said, the entrance to the canal from the Mediterranean Sea.
https://commons.wikimedia.org/wiki/File:Suez_Canal,_Port_Said_-_ISS_2.jpg

Things continued in this fashion for nearly nine decades until 1956, when Egypt elected Gamal Abdel Nasser as the country's second president.

Since 1954, the Egyptian military had been talking to the British about bringing an end to their colonial-era military presence in the canal zone. Egypt had also been handling sporadic battles with Israel along its borders.

When Nasser came to power, one of the first things he did was nationalize the Suez Canal with funds and weapons provided by Russia.

Several factors went into this decision. Nasser believed that nationalizing such an important asset was a good way of asserting Egypt's sovereignty and strengthening the nation's political position. He also felt that Egypt could benefit from the significant revenue the canal generated, especially as the country was struggling economically. This revenue could be used to fund other economic development projects.

Perhaps most importantly, Nasser hoped the nationalization of the Suez Canal would be the catalyst needed to unite the Arab world. He was a huge proponent of pan-Arabism. His vision for the Arab world was to unite them all under one political entity. Nasser felt the West had too much influence and control over the Middle East and that the best way to challenge that was to promote pan-Arabism.

President Gamal Abdel Nasser in 1966.
https://commons.wikimedia.org/wiki/File:Nasser1966.jpg

In response to Nasser's move, France, Britain, and Israel planned an armed attack against Egypt. The first blow came from Israel on October 29th, 1956, and on October 31st, the Israelites were joined by French and British forces.

Russia was eager to get a piece of the Middle East and saw Arab nationalism as the perfect way to do that. As soon as the countries attacked Egypt, Nikita Khrushchev, the leader of the Soviet Union, issued a stern warning to them, threatening to bring out nuclear missiles if they didn't leave Egypt.

Cold War tensions were already at a high, and this was the last thing the United States wanted. Both Russia and the US swiftly condemned the invasion, and the United Nations passed a resolution to bring an immediate end to the crisis.

American President Dwight D. Eisenhower was especially frustrated at Britain for taking such reckless and impulsive actions without speaking to the US first.

Bowing to American pressure, the three countries withdrew and gave up control of the canal. A peacekeeping mission from the United Nations was sent to make sure the withdrawal was conducted peacefully, and the crisis came to an end on November 7th, 1956.

Nasser emerged from the international incident as a hero. However, for the British, the humiliating defeat exposed their military limitations and was further proof that the empire was a declining world power with little influence on global matters. Being rebuked by the United Nations and being lectured by the United States were difficult things for the country to accept.

The Suez Canal crisis became a major turning point in British history. It marked the end of an era for British imperialism and signaled the start of a new world order led by Russia and the US.

Today, the canal is operated by the Suez Canal Authority of Egypt and continues to be one of the most used shipping lanes in the world.

Decolonization

In the aftermath of WWII, there was a significant shift toward decolonization, with cries for independence becoming more persistent.

Britain and other European powers were faced with increasing pressure from all sides to grant self-determination and independence to their colonies. International organizations like the United Nations played a key role in promoting decolonization and influencing colonial powers. This call for independence was further aided by growing awareness of different cultures and races and a rejection of imperialist attitudes and ideologies.

Economic challenges in the post-WWII period made it difficult for colonial powers to maintain their empires. The emergence of economic powers like the United States challenged the needs and dominance of imperial powers.

The dynamics of the Cold War were also a contributing factor for decolonization, as both the United States and Russia competed to gain influence and build alliances with new nations.

Each region had its own specific causes and reasons to decolonization. Earlier in this chapter, we briefly looked at why India was seeking independence. Ireland, another one of Britain's colonies, sought self-determination for similar reasons.

Irish nationalism and social unrest played a key role in Ireland's decolonization, with Irish nationalists pushing for a separate state. They felt that ongoing religious differences between the predominantly Catholic Irish and the Protestant minority and economic conditions like unemployment and poverty would be improved if Ireland was allowed to be independent and in charge of its own future.

But how did decolonization take place?

The process of decolonization and the formation of new nations was not an easy one. It involved a range of political, economic, and social changes, and it was frequently followed by a period of conflict, social unrest, and political upheaval.

It was difficult for a colonial power to cede control, and it was equally difficult for the new nation to navigate uncharted territory. In many cases, treaties or terms of independence were negotiated between a colonial power and the nationalist leader of a colony. These terms helped to establish constitutional reforms, which paved the way for decolonization.

When negotiating Ireland's independence, the British government and Irish representatives signed the Anglo-Irish Treaty. The terms of the treaty established the Irish Free State, which would be self-governed but still remain within the British Empire, like the Dominion of Canada. This happened on December 6th, 1921.

More than two decades later, on April 18th, 1949, Ireland made the decision to leave the Commonwealth and formally became a republic.

Decolonization in South Africa

In South Africa, the decolonization process was slightly more complicated due to apartheid and was achieved through three phases. South Africa initially gained independence before WWI on May 31st, 1910, but it stayed under British influence until 1961, at which point it finally became a republic.

However, true independence was limited because of apartheid. The legal system of forced racial segregation and discrimination against black South Africans became a serious point of contention for South Africa's independence.

The nation's actions were condemned internationally. Countries like Nigeria and Sudan and other organizations imposed economic sanctions on South Africa or refused to do business with it as a rebuke for apartheid. This worsened South Africa's already faltering economy.

Resistance movements like the African National Congress (ANC) continued to fight fiercely for decolonization and received international support.

Nelson Mandela, a key political figure of the anti-apartheid movement during this time, became heavily involved with the ANC, which had been banned by the government. His involvement in the armed struggle against apartheid led to his arrest in 1962. He spent twenty-seven years in prison, becoming a symbol of the anti-apartheid movement in the process. Mandela was also seen in the international world as an icon for human rights.

Increasing pressure was put on the South African government to change its apartheid policies, and in 1994, this finally happened. As part of the apartheid negotiations, Mandela was released from prison in 1990.

With the end of apartheid, thanks in large part to Mandela's tireless work, South Africa became a fully democratic country. The first elections held in the "new" country were open to every citizen, regardless of the color of their skin. To nobody's surprise, Mandela won the presidency and became South Africa's first black president.

Decolonization was a long, arduous process spanning many decades. The establishment of new nations marked a major shift in international power dynamics and led to decades of struggles over national identity, social justice, and other issues. Decolonization fundamentally changed the world.

The End of the Empire

Some historians argue that the British Empire ended as early as India's independence in 1947, while others believe the end came in 1997 with the handover of Hong Kong. Still, others view the formation of the Commonwealth of Nations as the defining moment when the British Empire was finished. The actual end is probably somewhere in the middle.

As we've seen above, Britain's global influence and control over its colonies sharply declined as the Second World War dragged on. In the postwar world, it became clear Britain had been displaced from its superpower role.

A surge of countries fighting for and achieving independence chipped away at the empire until all of its former glory and prestige had been stripped away. Colonies continued to gain independence into the 1950s and 1960s.

In 1979, Britain formally granted independence to Zimbabwe with the signing of the Lancaster House Agreement. The country held free and fair elections. The country's first black prime minister, Robert Mugabe, was elected, and Zimbabwe officially became a fully independent nation on April 18th, 1980. Zimbabwe was the last British colony in Africa to gain independence. Most historians argue the empire ended when Britain gave up Hong Kong.

Hong Kong had been seized by the British during the First Opium War. When China lost the war, peace was negotiated under the Treaty of Nanking in 1842. In this treaty, China officially ceded the territory of Hong Kong to Britain in perpetuity, and it became a crown colony. In 1860, after the Second Opium War, Britain further expanded the colony with the acquisition of the Kowloon Peninsula.

In 1898, Britain signed a ninety-nine-year lease for territories previously belonging to China. Hong Kong was part of that agreement. Britain ruled over Hong Kong until the ninety-nine years were up and handed the territory back to China.

With the handover, Britain's colonial rule in Hong Kong came to an official end. A treaty had been signed by the Chinese and the British in 1984, laying out the terms for the transfer. In the Sino-British Joint Declaration, China agreed to grant Hong Kong a high degree of autonomy. The people there were allowed to maintain their way of life, including a capitalist economy, and keep their way of governing separate from communist China.

The agreement was set for fifty years and should last until 2047. For decades, this arrangement has worked well, although recently, the Chinese government has increased its interference in Hong Kong's affairs and pushed its own communist agenda on it.

Today, there are fourteen British Overseas Territories around the globe. Most of them are smaller islands like Bermuda and the Cayman Islands.

Chapter 9: Key Figures from the Empire's History

The British Empire would not have been as impressive and powerful as it was without the contributions, leadership, and strategic thinking of thousands of personalities.

Every decision that led to the rise and fall of the empire was made by individuals who had a bigger vision of what the empire should be.

In this chapter, we will look at a few key figures from Britain's imperial history and examine their pivotal role in Britain's quest for dominance.

King Henry VII

January 28th, 1457–April 21st, 1509

King Henry VII is an important figure to mention in relation to the British Empire and its expansion.

He reigned from 1485 to 1509, and while he is not generally associated with having played a part in the building of the empire itself (the empire came into existence long after his reign was over), he did lay the groundwork for Britain to become a global superpower.

King Henry VII.

Henry VII initiated many policies and reforms that strengthened the country's economy, thus setting it up for future expansion. Before he came to the throne, the British monarchy was going through a very turbulent time, with conflicts and battles. When Henry took the throne, he ended the Wars of the Roses, which had left England destabilized for decades, with the House of Lancaster and the House of York fighting for the crown.

After King Edward V died in 1483, his uncle, Richard, Duke of Gloucester, seized the throne. Richard's reign was unpopular, and a rebellion soon broke out. Henry, who had strong supporters and a family lineage to support his claim for the throne, met Richard in battle. Legend has it that Henry VII picked up the crown from the battlefield as King Richard died, crowning himself king.

With Richard's death, the war, which had lasted for over thirty years, finally came to an end.

When Henry VII established the Tudor dynasty, a period of peace and stability in Britain followed.

Henry also reduced the power of the nobility while increasing the monarchy's authority. By doing this, he centralized power and created a more stable political system.

King Henry VII encouraged trade and commerce both at home and abroad by establishing trade agreements with European countries and other nations.

Aside from bringing stability back into the country, Henry VII's biggest contribution was his commission of expeditions to explore new trade routes. For example, in 1497, when John Cabot, the Italian navigator and explorer, set out to explore the New World, he did so under the commission of King Henry VII.

This voyage would become the first time since the Vikings that a European had set foot on mainland North America. Nothing concrete came out of that specific voyage, but the new lands would eventually become British colonies and then, eventually, the United States.

Henry VII died on April 21st, 1509, from tuberculosis.

While Henry himself did not contribute to the growth of the empire, King Henry VII, by creating a strong and economically stable country, provided Britain with the economic, political, and social resources to explore and conquer the world.

Sir Francis Drake

c. 1540-January 28th, 1596

Francis Drake was an English sea captain, explorer, and privateer who played an important role in the growth and expansion of the empire during the 16th century.

He is perhaps most famous for circumnavigating the globe. Drake started the expedition on December 15th, 1577. He crossed the Pacific Ocean and returned to England on September 26th, 1580.

The expedition earned him a knighthood from Queen Elizabeth I the following year. Seeing the potential for growth and trade with the New World through exploration, she granted him a privateer's commission. Drake was also granted permission to raid Spanish ships and settlements in the Americas, helping establish English dominance in the region.

Drake was one of the commanders of the English fleet who helped defeat the Spanish Armada in 1588. Repelling the Spanish invasion helped secure England's control of the seas, paving the way for the empire to become a powerful maritime force and promoting further expansion and colonization.

Sir Francis Drake, 1591.
https://commons.wikimedia.org/wiki/File:Gheeraerts_Francis_Drake_1591.jpg

Aside from his military contributions, Drake also helped England's economy by establishing trade relations with the Far East, as well as settlements in North America.

On his final voyage in 1596, he was headed for the West Indies. He contracted dysentery and died shortly after at sea. Drake's body was laid to rest in a lead coffin, and he was put out to sea. Despite many searches, his body has never been found.

While Sir Francis Drake was a key figure in the expansion of the empire, his legacy is quite complicated and clouded with some negatives.

For example, he was a slave trader, as was his cousin, John Hawkins. They attacked villages and slave ships to procure slaves, who were then sold to plantation owners. Drake treated Indigenous people in the Americas in a similar fashion, enslaving and exploiting them.

His actions as a privateer have also been critiqued for being unethical. The raids he was involved in came at a costly price since they involved acts of violence, brutality, and murder.

How one feels about Drake depends on where they stand on the idea of imperialism and colonization. Most people who had an impact on the British Empire were by no means perfect or without flaws. Oftentimes, they had to be ruthless and cutthroat to get what they wanted.

To some, Drake's actions helped make Britain the powerful empire it was, while to others, he was a man whose actions destroyed nations, cultures, and people.

Robert Clive

September 29ʰ, 1725–November 22ᵈ, 1774

One of the most important people involved in the expansion of the British Empire was Robert Clive. He played an especially important role in India, earning him the nickname Clive of India.

Robert Clive was born in England and was a difficult, troublesome boy. After trying a few different schools, Clive was sent to Madras (present-day Chennai) to serve in the British East India Company. He eventually entered into military service, where he finally found his calling.

In the ensuing years, he demonstrated his brilliant skills and military tactics. His most significant achievement was his victory at the Battle of Plassey in 1757. He led a small British force against the much larger army of the nawab of Bengal, who was also supported by French forces.

Against all odds, Clive's British troops won the Battle of Plassey, which cleared the way for the British to take control of Bengal and, eventually, other parts of India. This was the decisive battle that opened India up to Britain, and Clive was the man who achieved that victory.

Robert Clive was appointed governor of Bengal in 1758. He served again as governor between 1764 and 1767.

Under Clive's administration, the East India Company's position in India became stronger and one of the most powerful and profitable entities in the world. He achieved such success by imposing absolute control over the people and treating them with brutality.

Clive cruelly exploited India's people and the country's resources, and many of the problems the East India Company was condemned for, such as corruption, mismanagement, and mistreatment of people, were linked to his government.

He opened the floodgates of bribery and corruption when he accepted hundreds of thousands of pounds in cash and a noble Mughal title, among other things. Other officers in his government and the East India Company followed his lead. Corruption reached such uncontrollable levels that Bengal was almost ruined.

Clive died young. He was found at his home on November 22nd, 1774, with a self-inflicted gunshot wound. Historians speculate he might have committed suicide due to his failing health and increasing financial troubles.

The legacy he left behind is somewhat complicated. Some admire him for his military victories and his contributions to the empire, while others view him as an oppressor. Whichever way you may view him, his contribution to the British Empire's development and growth in India cannot be denied.

William Pitt

May 28th, 1759-January 23d, 1806

William Pitt is commonly referred to as William the Younger to differentiate him from his father, William Pitt, 1st Earl of Chatham, who played an important role during the Seven Years' War.

He is known for several things. One of the most interesting things is that he was the last prime minister of Great Britain and the first of the United Kingdom. This twist happened when Great Britain formally became known as the United Kingdom in January 1801. The change in name happened because of the Acts of Union of 1800, which united the kingdoms of Great Britain and Ireland.

Like his father, William the Younger was a prominent figure in British history during the late 18th and early 19th centuries. This was an especially turbulent time for Britain, as it was dealing with the revolution in North America and wars with Napoleon.

William Pitt the Younger served as Britain's prime minister twice, once from 1783 to 1801 and then again from 1804 to 1806. His policies and actions helped to shape British history and its position in the world. Pitt was a strong advocate for Britain's expansion and oversaw the acquisition of new territories like Australia and New Zealand.

During his time as prime minister, Pitt worked hard to strengthen Britain's military and economic position at home and abroad. He focused on reducing the government's spending and reforming the country's tax system.

Pitt felt that for the empire to stay strong, it needed to have a good relationship with its colonies, so he worked to strengthen ties with India and Canada. He was a strong supporter of the East India Company and championed reforms for the company to increase Britain's profitability.

The relationship between the American colonies and Britain was understandably strained after the American Revolution. Pitt recognized the importance of building a good relationship with the Americans and worked hard at improving it.

Strategic diplomacy helped to thaw the relationship, and trade and mutual economic interests forced the countries to work together. Over time, the two countries became strong allies and friends.

William Pitt was also a staunch supporter of the abolition of slavery, which began to take shape with the Slave Trade Act of 1807. This act put an end to the slave trade. It would take more time for the practice of slavery to be abolished entirely.

Portrait of William Pitt the Younger.
https://commons.wikimedia.org/wiki/File:OlderPittThe_Younger.jpg

Pitt's policies solidified Britain's control over its colonies and increased its influence globally at a critical point in the empire's expansion.

It's safe to assume that he would have done a lot more had his health not started declining in his early forties. He died on January 23rd, 1806, at just forty-six years old. He was given the rare honor of being buried in Westminster Abbey, which spoke volumes of how beloved he was in Britain.

Queen Victoria

May 24th, 1819-January 22nd, 1901

When Alexandrina Victoria was born, there was no reason to believe she would ever ascend the throne. Her father was the fourth son of King George III, and he had three older brothers who were in line for the throne. However, Victoria was destined to be queen, as her three uncles passed away without any legitimate heirs, making her the heir to the throne.

She became queen at eighteen years of age. She was young and relatively inexperienced; however, she proved to be a very capable and successful monarch. In 1840, she married Prince Albert of Saxe-Coburg and Gotha, who was her first cousin, and they had nine children together.

Coronation portrait of Queen Victoria.
https://en.wikipedia.org/wiki/File:Dronning_victoria.jpg

With over sixty-three years on the throne, Queen Victoria held the distinction of being the longest-reigning monarch in Britain until Queen Elizabeth II, who reigned for seventy years.

Queen Victoria came to the throne at an important time in Britain's history. The nation's power and influence were rapidly expanding, and the country was going through many social and political changes.

As a proud imperialist, Victoria played a key role in the consolidation of the empire and helped its expansion by supporting overseas exploration and colonization missions.

She was also a patron of numerous scientific and geographical societies and was instrumental in the development of industry and commerce in Britain. She oversaw the growth of the country's economy through the establishment of colonies and global trade agreements. Queen Victoria also created demand for British goods and products by promoting them through exhibitions like the Great Exhibition of 1851.

Great Exhibition of 1851.
https://commons.wikimedia.org/wiki/File:The_Crystal_Palace_in_Hyde_Park_for_Grand_Intern ational_Exhibition_of_1851.jpg

Britain's military was strengthened by Victoria. Under her reign, the British navy grew to become the largest and most powerful navy in the world.

Some notable expeditions during her time as queen included the explorations of Africa and India. After the British government took control of India after the Indian Rebellion of 1857, the country became a formal British colony.

In 1876, Queen Victoria was named empress of India. Working closely with the government, she worked to modernize and develop India's infrastructure. This included things like building railways, roads, and telegraph lines.

She was instrumental in pushing policies to integrate Indians into British customs and traditions. The educational system designed under her reign focused on teaching English and passing on British values.

While many of these changes and policies helped India, especially in regard to economic and technological advances, India suffered greatly. The native population was subject to exploitation and abuse, and there was a significant loss of India's traditional way of living, their customs, and their traditions. British values completely changed society.

Queen Victoria reigned until her death on January 22nd, 1901, and was succeeded by her son, Edward VII. She left behind an incredible legacy. The role she played as monarch helped Britain reach new heights of power and influence, and to this day, she is revered as one of the most influential monarchs in British history.

Joseph Chamberlain
July 8th, 1836-July 2nd, 1914

Joseph Chamberlain was a British politician, businessman, and statesman. Early in his career, he was an outspoken anti-imperialist, but his feelings evolved and changed over time. He eventually became a champion of imperialism.

Chamberlain was highly influential and had a significant impact on the empire's expansion during the late 19th and early 20th centuries. His political activities landed him the role of secretary of state for the colonies from 1895 to 1903. His role earned him the nickname "Empire Builder," as he was a key player in the governing of the British colonies, except for India and Canada.

Joseph Chamberlain.

Chamberlain's most important contribution to the empire was his support for imperial unity and greater cooperation and integration between Britain and its colonies. He advocated for policies that would strengthen that relationship and believed the empire could be used for good by promoting British values and interests.

Going hand in hand with this was his strong desire for free trade. He felt the empire would fare better economically if there was a system of economic cooperation and interdependence among the colonies. His economic policies were designed to do just that and became known as "Chamberlainism."

One of Chamberlain's most important policies was his support for imperial preference, which was a system where goods produced in British colonies would be subject to lower tariffs. Another key element of his economic policy was support for protectionism. He felt British industries should be protected from foreign competition, which could be done by imposing tariffs on imported goods and services. This would serve a dual purpose, as it would promote domestic manufacturing.

Chamberlain's policies were met with a lot of resistance from the colonies, as they wanted more independence from the Crown, not get closer to it.

Being a strong supporter of British involvement in South Africa, he played a key role in the country's expansion in Africa. He took part in the negotiations that eventually established British control over the region.

Chamberlain believed that Britain, as the "landlord" of the colonies, had a duty to develop territories, and he spent a lot of time and effort developing Africa and the West Indies, including founding the London School of Tropical Medicine in 1899.

Joseph Chamberlain died shortly before the start of the First World War on July 2nd, 1914, from a heart attack. He was offered a burial at Westminster Abbey, which his family refused.

While Chamberlain was admired by many, he also faced a lot of criticism. His critics felt he had failed to address the concerns of the native population or take them under consideration. But this was true of almost everyone who had a hand in the colonies. British interests were paramount and always came first.

The work Chamberlain did for the empire was incredibly important, and his policies shaped the trajectory of the empire. His legacy lives on in Britain.

His son, Neville Chamberlain, who served as prime minister of Britain from 1937 to 1940, was the one who declared war on Germany after Hitler's invasion. He led the country through the initial months of the war until his resignation on May 9th, 1940. He was succeeded by his colleague Winston Churchill, who would become one of the most influential people in British history.

Winston Churchill

November 30th, 1874-January 24th, 1965

Veteran, politician, orator, and painter—Winston Churchill was a man of various talents. He enjoyed a long and illustrious political career in Britain.

Winston Churchill came from an aristocratic and political family. His father, Lord Randolph Churchill, was a member of Parliament and a descendant of the 1st Duke of Marlborough.

Winston joined the Royal Military Academy as a cadet when he was nineteen years old, and within a few years, he expressed interest in politics and parliamentary affairs and began a career in government.

Churchill in military dress uniform.
https://commons.wikimedia.org/wiki/File:Winston_Churchill_1874_-_1965_ZZZ5426F.jpg

When WWI broke out, Churchill decided to join the army and fought in the trenches. Once the war was over, he went back to government and politics, becoming the secretary of state for the colonies in February 1921.

By this time, Churchill already had a very impressive resume. However, his most notable contribution to Britain was how he led the country through the Second World War.

After Prime Minister Neville Chamberlain resigned from the position, Winston took over. At that time, Britain was dealing with a powerful and seemingly unstoppable German army that was sweeping through Europe, conquering territories. Britain itself was facing the threat of a Nazi invasion.

Churchill in 1941.

https://en.wikipedia.org/wiki/File:Sir_Winston_Churchill_-_19086236948.jpg

Morale was low, and fear and anxiety gripped the nation. Churchill rallied the British people with his speeches and his determination to fight, even in the face of overwhelming odds. With his background in politics and with firsthand knowledge of war, he was likely the perfect person to be at the helm during this crisis.

Churchill's fearless leadership through some of the war's darkest battles and days, such as the Battle of Dunkirk and the Battle of Britain, are what he's most remembered for.

He was strong and inspiring. He was also a brilliant orator. Winston Churchill kept Britain united and focused on what was important during the war. His wartime speeches are viewed as some of the most powerful ones ever delivered.

Churchill's leadership played a key role in the Allied victory, as he worked closely with other Allied leaders like American President Franklin D. Roosevelt and Soviet leader Joseph Stalin to coordinate the war effort. Their combined resources, strategies, and meticulous planning led to the defeat of Hitler and the Nazis.

Despite being an extremely popular leader, Churchill lost the election in 1945, but he was reelected again in 1951.

Postwar, Churchill played a key role in the establishment of the United Nations and strongly believed that Europe should be united, especially as the continent faced a new threat from the Soviet Union and communism.

Churchill was a great advocate of social welfare policies and openly spoke out against apartheid in South Africa. He also has the distinction of enjoying a close friendship with Queen Elizabeth II, whom he had known since she was a child. They shared a special fondness for one another, and he played a key role in the organization of her coronation.

When he died at the age of ninety, he was given a state funeral, which was attended by dignitaries from around the world. In British and international history, he is widely viewed as a hero and one of the greatest wartime leaders of the 20th century.

Chapter 10: An Untouchable Legacy

Over the nine previous chapters, we've looked at how Britain evolved from an island nation into the most powerful empire in the world. And then how it began to shrink and fragment, getting weaker until it had virtually no power or influence at all.

As the country stands today, a developed, Westernized, democratic nation, we can ask ourselves if the country is still relevant in today's world. If so, how?

The short answer is yes. While Britain may not be as powerful as it once was, the nation continues to be a major player in international politics, economics, culture, and diplomacy. For centuries, Britain has been an influential leader on the world stage, and this continues to hold true.

Politically, Britain is involved in global affairs through memberships in international organizations like the United Nations and NATO. Britain used to be part of the European Union as well until Brexit in 2020.

Much like in the postwar decades, Britain continues to play a diplomatic peacekeeper role, focusing on promoting peace and stability in underdeveloped or conflict-ridden regions around the world. Britain is also a major donor of foreign aid and a leader in the fight against many challenges facing the globe today, like poverty, human rights, and climate change.

Britain's Second Empire?

At the time of publishing, a total of fifteen different countries still share the British monarch as the head of their state. They include the following:

1. United Kingdom
2. Canada
3. Australia
4. New Zealand
5. Papua New Guinea
6. Jamaica
7. The Bahamas
8. Grenada
9. Saint Kitts and Nevis
10. Saint Lucia
11. Antigua and Barbuda
12. Saint Vincent and the Grenadines
13. Solomon Islands
14. Tuvalu
15. Belize

Given the number of countries that still view the British monarch as their head of state, can a case be made to argue that Britain's second empire is still alive and thriving?

The answer is no. When Britain was an empire, it had direct control and ruled over the colonies. The countries that have Britain as their current head of state have no constitutional relationship with the United Kingdom. The monarch is a figurehead based on historical and constitutional ties.

Britain does retain a significant global presence and exerts a considerable amount of influence globally, but its power and reach do not come close to what it used to be when the empire was at its peak.

The decolonization process and national issues like Brexit, immigration, and politics have all dramatically reduced Britain's prestige and international reputation. The rise of other global powers like the United States and China has added an additional layer of challenge.

So, while Britain undoubtedly continues to be an important player in global affairs, it does not dominate or influence the world in any significant way, and there is no basis to claim that a second empire is in full swing.

It can be assumed the sun has set on the British Empire, but that does not mean it cannot once again be a superpower. However, first, the nation has to heal itself and decide what kind of country it wants to be.

Britain Today

The world's sixth-largest economy as of this writing belongs to Britain, an industrialized, democratic, and developed nation. Yet, the Bank of England predicts the country is about to see its steepest decline in living standards ever.

Once on par with the most powerful economies of the world, experts state Britain's economy is more comparable to those of weaker Eastern European nations today. It's a problem that will likely only continue to get worse.

Britain seems to be going through a great social and political upheaval as it struggles to navigate an increasingly desperate economic situation.

After centuries of being assured of its position in the world, the country went through some major shifts after WWII. It lost its entire empire, political stature, most of its influence, and its economic and political strength.

It's no secret that Britain has been floundering and facing a number of challenges and uncertainties, including geopolitical shifts and a struggling economy, which, in turn, is having a big impact on social and environmental issues.

Britain's economic crisis has been going on for some time now and has been made worse with the pandemic. Everything has been compounded by the soaring cost of living, high interest rates, taxes, and inflation.

Nearly a third of Britain's children live in poverty. Hundreds of thousands of households live on Social Security checks and are unable to regularly put food on the table. Millions more are mired in debt and struggling to stay afloat financially.

For a significant percentage of the population, Britain feels like a broken country where they will eventually either starve or freeze to death. It's a sad state of affairs for this once-glorious empire.

In early 2023, the Office for National Statistics said the nation's economy was stagnant for the last quarter of 2022 and that the average middle-class family could expect to see their incomes fall by nearly 13 percent.

Britain is the only major economy in the world that seems not to have fully recovered post-pandemic. A significant drop in trade with the European Union due to increased taxes for businesses and consumers is also having a negative impact on the nation's economy. Customer spending has decreased, which is bad for businesses and the economy.

According to the International Monetary Fund (IMF), Britain is the only advanced nation whose economy will decline in 2023; it is expected to shrink by 0.6 percent.

Britain is also experiencing significant challenges with labor shortages. When the pandemic first hit, Britain's economy was hit harder than most countries, and its access to workers and skilled laborers has become very limited since Brexit since they no longer have a pool of European workers. This, in turn, has made for a sluggish, rigid, and less resilient economy.

Like a vicious cycle, the crumbling economy is having a severe impact on public services and society. Education standards are decreasing, physical and mental health issues are increasing, and the government seems unable or powerless to help. In short, Britain is going through a significant crisis with no real end in sight.

Britain seems lost and unsure of its place in the world, which cannot be wholly unexpected. The British appear to be trying to balance the past with the present and reconcile who they were and what they lost with who they want to be.

The struggle seems to lay in trying to find an identity in a world that is wholly foreign to them. It must be difficult playing a lesser role when, for centuries, the nation had always been the unquestioned leader. It cannot be easy watching the United States, once a former colony, upstaging them on every level.

Is it possible for Britain to regain some of its former glory? Can it, like a phoenix, rise from the ashes?

That could certainly happen, but in order to do so, Britain must let go of the past it clings to so desperately and embrace the new order of things. The nation has to learn to modernize, change, and evolve.

Brexit

Many people feel that Britain's economy has spiraled downward quickly since Brexit. Brexit refers to Britain's highly controversial decision to leave the European Union (EU).

What is the European Union? It's a political and economic union of twenty-seven member states from western, eastern, and central Europe. The union's existence is rooted in several treaties that were drafted post-WWII. The idea was to build economic cooperation with one another and link their economies to avoid future conflicts.

Additional objectives of the EU include promoting peace, democracy, and economic prosperity. A number of institutions fall within the EU, including the European Parliament, the European Council, and the European Commission. They each serve a different purpose but have one main aim: cooperation.

Membership to the EU is purely voluntary.

For some time, the British had been feeling that belonging to the EU was holding them back from having control over their own laws and policies. For example, Britain wanted to slow down the number of immigrants being allowed into the country, but it couldn't do so because of EU immigration policies. The British felt similar frustrations regarding trade; Britain felt the policies of the EU were preventing them from negotiating better deals with other countries. There was also concern about the amount of money Britain was contributing to the EU, with arguments being made that leaving the EU would be a big money saver.

In short, supporters of Brexit believed that leaving the EU would allow Britain to regain control of its borders, reduce bureaucracy, and make its own laws, mainly around immigration and trade. Those who were against it argued that the move would damage the country's economy, weaken its international standing, and reduce opportunities for trade and cooperation with other EU member states.

After years of speculation and discussion, a referendum was held on the matter. Nearly 52 percent of the voters chose to leave the EU.

Negotiations between the EU and Britain were complicated and dragged on for several years, with the country formally leaving the EU on January 31st, 2020.

The full effects of Brexit are still unknown, but the immediate aftermath has been less than stellar. Economically, Britain's departure has meant new tariffs and trade barriers that have impacted the nation's ability to trade and invest with the EU and other countries with the same ease as before.

Politically, it has created great upheaval, with Prime Minister David Cameron resigning soon after the referendum and Boris Johnson taking office. His time as prime minister was mired with scandal and negativities. The outcome of Brexit has also increased tensions between Britain, Scotland, and Northern Island, as they are now being forced to deal with the consequences of Brexit.

Socially, it has created a lot of unhappiness within the British population, many of whom feel that Britain is going backward instead of forward.

It's too soon to tell whether Brexit was a mistake or not. If the country manages to sort out the issues that have arisen from leaving the EU, Britain may become a stronger and more powerful country.

However, in a world that is increasingly interlinked, where the prosperity and development of a nation is reliant on cooperation and strong alliances, one wonders why Britain would make such a decision. Was it pride? A desire to be the fearless, independent nation it once was? An empire that was a leader and not a follower?

Whatever the reason, Britain is at a crossroads right now, and the next steps it takes will determine what kind of country it will become in the next decades.

The Silver Linings of the Empire

The British Empire has obviously courted a lot of controversy and negativity. The nation has been condemned for many of its actions against the colonies. However, it cannot be denied that the British Empire contributed a lot of positive things to the world as well.

Britain's empirical reign led to English becoming the universal language. Most of the world speaks and communicates fairly easily in English, and most of us do it without a thought. We take our ability to communicate with many parts of the world in English for granted.

But would that have happened if Britain had never built an empire? The British spread their language, culture, and values to their colonies. What would the universal language be today if Britain hadn't done that?

Also, would globalization have come later? Would the world feel like a much larger place than it does today without Britain creating and establishing trade links and routes?

Trade allows us to sit in one country while enjoying food, beverages, and goods from another. Would it be so easily accessible today without the British? Can it be argued that Britain's rule over the world expedited this process?

Without a doubt, the outcome of the Second World War would have been quite different without the British Empire. We can't say definitively that Hitler would have won the war, but a strong argument can be made that he could have.

During the period of colonization when empires were rushing to conquer colonies, if Britain had chosen not to colonize, many of the British colonies would likely have ended up in the hands of other empires, including Germany and Russia. That alone would have changed the face of both world wars completely.

Britain had strong support from its allies during the war, most of them colonies or, in the case of the United States, former colonies. As we know, the United States played a critical role in helping the Allies achieve victory during both global conflicts, and its entire existence is because of the British Empire and its push for imperialism.

If Britain hadn't conquered and colonized (and been so insufferable), the Thirteen Colonies might never have revolted. Each little thing that happened centuries ago has rippled into the world we live in today. America is a superpower today because of the American Revolution.

On the flip side, what if America had been colonized by one of the Axis Powers instead? The Nazis could have potentially won. Communism could have won. The world we live in today would have been radically different if that had happened. Instead of enjoying the rights and freedoms afforded by democratic Western nations, most of the world could have been living under authoritarian regimes.

Worse still, we might have gone through a third world war.

Conclusion

It can be argued the world would have been a radically different place if Britain had never aspired to be an empire. Assuming everything else in history unfolded as it did (for instance, Hitler's rise to power, the Cold War, etc.), what would the world be like without Britain's dominance and strength?

What would life have been like for nations in Africa, Asia, and the Middle East? Would they be mired in conflict, turn into wealthy developed nations, or belong to someone else entirely? While we may never be able to answer these questions, it's interesting to speculate on what could have been.

We've taken an in-depth look at how Britain's influence has dramatically fallen since the mid-20th century, but could it one day be a match for the superpowers of today? Or even overtake them entirely? The answer is likely no.

The British Empire has proved that it is strong, resilient, and resourceful. It may be premature to write it off completely as rising to match the superpowers of today, but given the number of problems the country is facing, including a housing crisis, a dramatic rise in unemployment, and economic struggles, it can be safely assumed that Britain has a long way to go before it reaches superpower status again.

Part of getting there is to modernize, understand the people, and let go of the past. The country needs to be more open to immigration as a way of stimulating growth and filling the labor gaps.

Britain may also need to consider what purpose the monarchy serves. Most European nations have given up on monarchies, considering them outdated institutions, or changed the way the institution functions to be more in line with the demands of present-day realities.

Britain places significant importance on the royal family, tying its national identity to the existence of the institution. However, the truth of the matter is the British monarchy is perhaps one of the most controversial monarchies, and the fact that the royal family seems so out of touch with the real world doesn't help Britain's reputation.

In recent years, a number of controversies surrounding the royal family, like Prince Harry and Meghan Markle's marriage and the fall-out that occurred, as well as the scandal with Prince Andrew and his relationship with Epstein, has left the monarchy on shakier grounds than it has been in a very long time.

Many people are finding it difficult to accept Camilla by King Charles's side since the specter of Diana hangs over them.

While some people eagerly looked forward to the coronation, seeing it as a chance for Britain to showcase its might and tradition, many found it difficult to comprehend how King Charles could organize a coronation that cost taxpayers over $125 million, especially at a time when people are struggling to find food or keep a roof over their heads.

The younger generation, in particular, is increasingly questioning the need for a royal family whose lives are funded by taxpayer money and a monarchy that has been built on the backs of slavery.

There are increasing demands from some former colonies to have stolen jewels returned to them, and several Commonwealth nations have indicated their intention to become republics in the upcoming years.

King Charles III's coronation on May 6th, 2023, saw hundreds of anti-monarchy protestors booing the king and chanting for the abolition of the monarchy.

If these sentiments and tensions from within and abroad continue to rise, will the monarchy be able to survive for another century? Or even another generation?

It's a well-known fact that Charles does not enjoy the same popularity or command the same respect as his mother did. Can the monarchy exist if the people choose to no longer bow down to it? Will getting rid of the monarchy make Britain more modern? Some believe it can since most of the monarchies around the world have been abolished. Others don't see the relevance since the king has no official decision-making power in politics and is simply a figurehead. Whatever the case may be, one thing is clear: the concept of a monarchy continues to divide British society, and some big changes may come about as a result.

Britain is not the nation it once was, and the problem is it keeps wanting to be. Instead of dwelling on its time in the sun, Britain needs to consider how it can learn from its history and legacy to become an even greater power in the generations to come.

Here's another book by Enthralling History that you might like

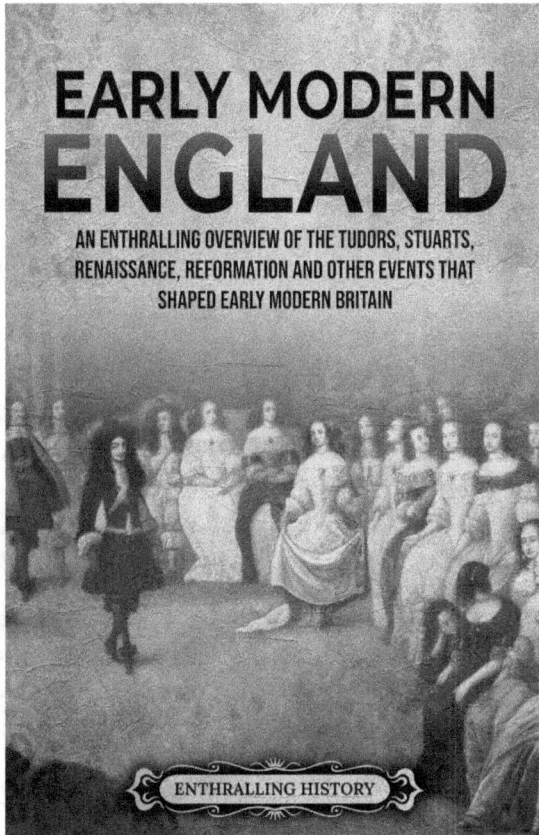

EARLY MODERN ENGLAND

AN ENTHRALLING OVERVIEW OF THE TUDORS, STUARTS, RENAISSANCE, REFORMATION AND OTHER EVENTS THAT SHAPED EARLY MODERN BRITAIN

ENTHRALLING HISTORY

Free limited time bonus

Stop for a moment. We have a free bonus set up for you. The problem is this: we forget 90% of everything that we read after 7 days. Crazy fact, right? Here's the solution: we've created a printable, 1-page pdf summary for this book that you're reading now. All you have to do to get your free pdf summary is to go to the following website:

https://livetolearn.lpages.co/enthrallinghistory/

Once you do, it will be intuitive. Enjoy, and thank you!

We forget 90% of everything
that we've read in 7 days...

Get the free printable pdf summary of
the book you've read AND much, much
more... shhhh...

Enter Your Most Frequently Used Email to Get Started

**DOWNLOAD FREE PDF
SUMMARY**

© Enthralling History

Sources

"British Empire." https://www.britannica.com/place/British-Empire.

"'Crowning the Coloniser': Early origins, 1175-1603." https://museumofbritishcolonialism.org/2023-4-16-monarchy-and-empire-origins/

Ferguson, Niall. *Empire: How Britain Made the Modern World.* 2018.

James, Lawrence. *The Rise and Fall of the British Empire.* 1997.

Tharoor, Shasi. *Inglorious Empire: What the British Did to India.* 2018.